Easy Chinese Cooking

TARLA DALAL

India's #1 Cookery Author

S&C

SANJAY & CO.

MUMBAI

Other Books by Tarla Dalal

INDIAN COOKING
Tava Cooking
Rotis & Subzis
Desi Khana
The Complete Gujarati Cook Book
Mithai
Chaat
Achaar aur Parathe
The Rajasthani Cookbook
Swadisht Subzian

TOTAL HEALTH
Low Calorie Healthy Cooking
Pregnancy Cookbook
Baby and Toddler Cookbook
Cooking with 1 Teaspoon of Oil
Home Remedies
Delicious Diabetic Recipes
Fast Foods Made Healthy
Healthy Soups & Salads
Healthy Breakfast
Calcium Rich Recipes
Healthy Heart Cook Book
Forever Young Diet
Healthy Snacks

WESTERN COOKING
The Complete Italian Cookbook
The Chocolate Cookbook
Eggless Desserts
Mocktails & Snacks
Soups & Salads
Mexican Cooking
Easy Gourmet Cooking
Chinese Cooking
Thai Cooking
Sizzlers & Barbeque

Iron Rich Recipes
Healthy Juices
Low Cholesterol Recipes
Good Food for Diabetes
Healthy Subzis
Healthy Snacks for Kids
High Blood Pressure Cook Book
Low Calorie Sweets
Nutritious Recipes for Pregnancy
Diabetic Snacks
Zero Oil Rotis & Subzis New
Zero Oil Soups, Salads & Snacks New
Zero Oil Dal-Chawal New
Acidity Cookbook New

MINI SERIES
Idlis & Dosas
Cooking under 10 minutes
Pizzas and Pasta
Fun Food for Children
Roz Ka Khana
Microwave - Desi Khana
T.V. Meals
Paneer
Parathas
Chawal
Dals

Sandwiches
Quick Cooking
Curries & Kadhis
Chinese Recipes
Jain Desi Khana
7 Dinner Menus
Jain International Recipes
Punjabi Subzis
Corn
Microwave Subzis
Baked Dishes New
Stir-Fry New

GENERAL COOKING
Exciting Vegetarian Cooking
Microwave Recipes
Quick & Easy Cooking
Saatvik Khana
Mixer Cook Book
Ice-creams & Frozen Desserts
The Pleasures of Vegetarian Cooking
The Delights of Vegetarian Cooking
The Joys of Vegetarian Cooking
Cooking with Kids
Snacks Under 10 Minutes
Desserts Under 10 Minutes
Entertaining
Microwave Snacks & Desserts

Fourth Printing : 2007

ISBN 10 : 81-86469-76-1
ISBN 13 : 978-8-186469-76-7

Price Rs. 230/-

Published & distributed by
SANJAY & COMPANY
A-1, 353 Shah & Nahar Industrial Estate, Dhanraj Mill Compound, Lower Parel (W), Mumbai 400 013, INDIA.
Tel: (91-22) 2496 8068 / Fax: (91-22) 2496 5876 / Email: sanjay@tarladalal.com / Website: www.tarladalal.com

UK and USA customers can call us on :
UK : 02080029533 • USA : 213-634-1406
For books, Membership on **tarladalal.com**, Subscription for **Cooking & More** and Recipe queries
Timing : 9.30 a.m. to 7.00 p.m. (IST), from Monday to Saturday
Local call charges applicable

Recipe Research &
Production Design
Pinky Dixit
Pradyna Sundararaj

Photography
Sandeep Mhatre

Cover Image
Vinay Mahidhar

Design
Satyamangal Rege

Marketing Consultant
Harbinder Bindra, Addvalue International

Printed by :
Minal Sales Agencies, Mumbai

Food Stylist
Nitin Tandon

A large number of people have begun to enjoy traditional Chinese cooking, making it one of the most popular cuisines the world over.

It is no longer the preserve of the ethnic Chinese; and a sizeable number of people around the world have now become highly competent, if not expert, in preparing Chinese dishes.

The Chinese believe that to achieve bodily harmony, one must balance the intake of yin (cool, bland) foods with yang (the rich and hot) foods.

Chinese cooking strives for balance, both nutritive and aesthetic. It is pleasing to the eye and also a fragrant marriage of flavours and textures.

Although it is laborious to prepare the ingredients, the actual cooking takes only a few minutes which ensures that the food is cooked to perfection, retaining all the fresh flavours and the end result is something that pleases all senses.

I have included a small section on the various ways of preparing and cutting the ingredients in the authentic Chinese way.

Like India, China is a vast country with pronounced differences in regional cuisines. The main food areas of China are Peking, Tianjin, Shanghai and Guangzhou (Canton).

I have enjoyed elaborate vegetarian banquets in all of these regions and have discovered that the Cantonese and the Schezuan styles of cooking continue to remain the most appealing to the Indians. This is because the sauces and spices are more attuned to the Indian palate and this book is accordingly based on these styles.

You can be as creative as you like with no limit to the number of dishes you can prepare using the ingredients you may have handy or will find easily in most provision stores and supermarkets.

Also included is a glossary which throws light on those ingredients that we are not very familiar with and which are essential as they bring out the authentic flavours in Chinese cooking.

The recipes in this book use locally available ingredients that are easy to procure and I have also made appropriate recommendations for substituting ingredients that are difficult to find.

I hope you enjoy cooking these recipes as much as I did…

HAPPY COOKING !!

Regards,

Tarla Dalal

- Chinese Cooking Basics -

China is a country where the preparation and appreciation of food has been developed to the highest level. Chinese culture considers cooking *an art*. All other philosophies consider the preparation of food a *craft*.

The two dominant philosophies of the Chinese culture are Confucianism and Taoism. Each influenced the course of Chinese history and the development of the culinary arts.

Taoism was responsible for the development of the hygienic aspects of foods and cooking. The principal objects of this philosophy were nourishment of the body and the search for longevity.

In contrast to Confucianists who were interested in the taste, texture and appearance, Taoists were concerned with the life-giving attributes of various foods.

The tradition of cutting foods into bite size pieces during preparation and not at the table is unique to the Chinese culture. The use of knives at a Chinese dinner is considered "poor taste", therefore chopsticks reign.

Illustrated below are a few simple ways to prepare all your ingredients correctly so that your Chinese cooking is deliciously authentic.

- Cutting -

It is important to remember that cutting before cooking introduces harmony as well as brings out the true flavours of the ingredients. Thinly cut food requires only a short cooking time, and the natural flavours are thus preserved.

The food should be cut into units of roughly the same *shape, size and thickness*.

thickness. If the main ingredient of a recipe is shredded, then so are the other ingredients. Use a sharp knife or invest in a Chinese cleaver for best results.

The four basic cutting methods are as follows:

Slicing - the ingredients are cut into thin slices. The thickness depends on what is specified in each individual recipe.

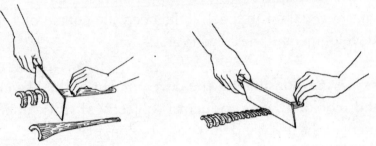

Diagonal cutting - this method is normally used for cutting vegetables such as asparagus, carrots, celery or french beans. The cleaver is held diagonally across the ingredient to be cut which is then sliced diagonally.

Shredding - the ingredients are stacked like a pack of playing cards, and then cut into thin strips. Spinach, lettuce, cabbage are all shredded.

Dicing - The ingredients are first cut into strips as wide as they are thick, then the strips are cut at right angles in the same width so they become cubes.

- Cooking -

The various methods of cooking can be divided into four main categories: viz. *stir frying, braising, stewing, deep frying and steaming.*

Besides these methods the Chinese also parboil and blanch foods which help in the pre-preparation of food, so as to reduce the time taken to finish the actual cooking.

- Parboil -

To parboil means, to partially cook food by boiling it briefly in water. This is a timesaving technique used for vegetables such as carrots, baby corn etc which take a long time to cook. If parboiled, the vegetables can be added at the last minute with quick-cooking ingredients (such as bean sprouts and celery) in preparations like <u>stir-fries</u>. Parboiling ensures that all the ingredients complete cooking at the same time.

- Blanch -

Blanching means plunging food (usually vegetables and fruits) into boiling water for a very short time, and then into cold water to stop the cooking process.

Blanching is used to loosen skins (as with peaches and tomatoes) and also to heighten the colour and flavour (for example, blanching spinach).

- Stir Frying -

While the Chinese use various cooking methods, their unique contribution to the culinary arts is **Stir Frying**. A Chinese immigrant to the United States described the process as, "a big fire- shallow fat - continuous stirring- quick frying of cut up ingredients with wet seasoning.". Funny as it may sound....stir frying is just that!

Stir fry is a great way to put together a quick main dish that's low in fat, high in nutrition and takes advantage of a new approach to eating that helps protect against chronic diseases. Prepared properly, a stir fry is low in calories and fat.

The food to be cooked is first cut into uniform bite sized pieces so as to ensure that maximum surface area is exposed to heat while stir frying, thus cooking the food quickly and evenly.

Contd...

How to stir fry?

Heat up the oil in a pre-heated wok over a high heat, throw in the ingredients and constantly stir and toss them for a short time.

Timing is of the utmost importance: overcooking will turn the food into a soggy mess. When correctly done, the *food should be crispy and wholesome*.

Very little water is added, or none at all, since the high heat will bring out the natural juices from the ingredients, particularly if they are fresh.

Use good quality ingredients that are fresh for best results, as the final product depends entirely on the quality of raw ingredients used. Since most of the stir fried recipes use very few seasoning and flavouring agents, the flavours of the staple ingredients dominate the dish.

One must be able to control the heat with perfect ease, as it is vital to turn it down or bring it up at the crucial moments during the cooking process. If the heat is too high for too long, the food will be either overcooked or burnt outside and raw inside. A little bit of practice will guide you when to fluctuate the heat during the cooking process.

Another important factor in stir frying is the pan called a 'wok' in which it is actually done. It is interesting to note that the whole spectrum of Chinese cooking methods can be executed in one single utensil, namely the **wok**.

- Chinese utensils -

Traditionally, the Chinese ingenuity is seen in their basic cooking utensils - the wok and the cleaver which the Chinese cooks use with great skill and speed.

- The Wok -

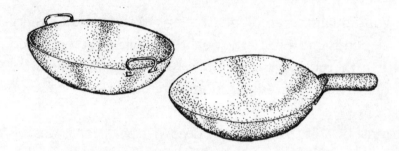

The wok was designed with a rounded bottom to fit snugly over a traditional Chinese brazier or oven, which burns wood or charcoal. It conducts and retains heat evenly, and because of the conical shape the food always returns to the centre where the heat is most intense. For this reason it is ideally suited for quick stir frying.

When it comes to deep frying, the conical shaped wok requires far less oil than a flat-bottomed deep fryer, and it has more depth (which means more heat) and more frying surface (which means more food can be cooked more quickly at one go).

Furthermore, since the wok has a larger capacity at the top than at the base, when the oil level rises as the raw ingredients are added there is little chance of the oil overflowing and causing the pan to catch fire as often happens with a conventional deep-fryer.

There are models made with steel, aluminum, copper, Teflon,

porcelainized enamel, with coloured exteriors etc., All these are specifically designed and manufactured for the Western market. Choose one that suits your needs and your budget, although the iron ones are not only reasonably priced but are also easier to maintain.

When you have cooked in a new iron wok for at least eight to ten times, and if you do not wash it with detergents or metal abrasives, it will acquire a beautiful, glossy finish like a well-seasoned omelette pan. This is much treasured by Chinese cooks as 'wok flavour'. Simply wipe the wok with a damp cloth and then a dry one before putting it away.

Besides being a frying pan (deep or shallow), the wok is also used for braising, steaming, boiling and even smoking.

- The Chinese Cleaver (Chopper) -

A Chinese cleaver may appear to the uninitiated as hefty and ominously sharp. But in reality it is quite light, steady, and not at all dangerous to use as long as it is used correctly and with caution and care.

Once you have learnt to regard it as a kitchen tool mainly used for cutting and not just a chopper, then you will be surprised how easy and simple it is to use compared to an ordinary knife.

Chinese cleavers - are not the same as those used in Western cooking and are available in a variety of materials and weights. Choose one made of tempered carbon steel with a wood handle. Ideally it should be neither too heavy nor too light, but should be a medium weight dual-purpose cleaver known as the 'civil and military knife' (wen-wu dao in Chinese).

How to use a cleaver

The lighter, front half of the blade is used for slicing, shredding, scoring etc;
The heavier, rear half of the blade is used for chopping and so on. You can also use the back of the blade as a pounder and tenderizer,
The flat side of the blade is used for crushing and transporting; while the end of the handle can even used as a pestle for grinding spices etc.

Some of the ingredients used in this book may be quite a mystery to many of us. I know I was quite baffled with some of them when I had started experimenting with Chinese cooking…. I list below some of the ingredients I have used in this book.

- Vegetables -

Bean Sprouts

Bean Sprouts are tender sprouts of the Moong (mung) bean. For optimum flavour and crispness, sprouts are best eaten raw. Sprouts are also stir fried or sautéed, but should only be cooked for 30 seconds or less as prolonged cooking will wilt them. Bean Sprouts should be refrigerated in a plastic bag for no more than 3 days.
They are easily available at most provision stores and vegetable vendors and can all be made at home by soaking and sprouting moong beans. This will take approximately 36 hours in warm weather.

Celery

Celery is a plant with light green stalks and dark green leaves. Apart from being used abundantly in most Chinese dishes it is also used in continental cooking to impart a distinct flavour to the food. Only the stalks are used in cooking. The leaves are usually discarded but can also be used to flavour stocks.
It is easily available at most vegetable vendors.

Dried Black Mushrooms (Shitake)

Dried black mushrooms are commonly known as Shitake mushrooms or Chinese mushrooms. They are dark brown in colour and have a full bodied flavour. The stems are extremely tough and are therefore to be discarded. They have to be soaked in warm water for at least 20 minutes before use. After the mushrooms are soaked, the stems have to be broken and discarded and the heads can then be used as required.

Snow Peas (Mangetout)

These are from the pea family and are used in cooking just like we use French beans.
The fact that this vegetable is entirely edible including the pod accounts for its French name *"mange-tout"*, or "eat it all." It is an almost translucent, bright green pod that is thin and crisp. The tiny seeds inside are tender and sweet. Both tips of a snow pea should be broken off just before using. Snow peas are also called *Chinese snow peas.*
They are easily available at most vegetable vendors during the winter.

Pakchoi

Pakchoi is a variety of Chinese cabbage and is also known as spoon cabbage because the leaves are spoon shaped. This plant has dark green leaves with a white stalk and is an excellent vegetable for stir frying. Both the stalk and the leaves can be used.

It is easily available ready made in bottles at most vegetable vendors.

- Other Ingredients -

Black Bean Sauce

This sauce is made from fermented black beans and has a pungent and salty flavour. The black bean sauce is a proprietory product and cannot be made at home. It is available ready made in bottles, at most leading supermarkets.

Hoisin Sauce

Hoisin sauce a thick, reddish-brown sauce which is sweet and spicy. It is widely used in Chinese cooking. It's a mixture of soybeans, garlic, peppers and various spices and is easily available at leading provision stores.
Once opened, canned hoisin should be transferred to a non-metal container, tightly sealed and refrigerated. Bottled hoisin sauce can be refrigerated as is. Both will keep indefinitely when stored in this manner.

Vegetarian Oyster Sauce

A dark-brown sauce consisting of vegetable extracts, brine and soya sauce cooked until thick and concentrated. Oyster sauce imparts a richness to dishes without overpowering their natural flavour. It is available at most leading provision stores.

Chinese 5 Spice Powder

This mixture of five ground spices is slightly sweet and pungent. Star anise, cinnamon, clove, Schezuan pepper and fennel are the five spices used to make this powder. Store tightly covered, in a dry place at room temperature. I have added a recipe on page 146.

Ajinomoto (Mono Sodium Glutamate)

Ajinomoto is a flavouring agent used extensively in the Chinese cuisine. A Japanese firm first sold it under the name Ajinomoto meaning "prime element of taste" and since then mono sodium glutamate has been synonymous with the name Ajinomoto.

Ajinomoto helps to enhance the taste of food and is made mostly from gluten of flour.

Recently, there have been many controversies regarding its usage. I would recommend that children and pregnant women avoid eating it even at restaurants.

I have omitted it in many of these recipes and have added it only as an option, in some recipes.

Rice Noodles

These extremely thin Chinese noodles resemble long, translucent white hairs. When deep fried, they explode dramatically into a tangle of airy, crunchy strands that are used for garnish. Rice noodles are also used in soups and stir fries. They are usually sold in coiled nests packaged in cellophane and are easily available at most provision stores.

They have to be soaked in hot water for 10 minutes and then drained before use a recipe.

Bean Curd (Tofu)

Bean curd is made from soya bean milk and has a very distinct flavour and smell. It is very perishable and should be kept submerged in water in a refrigerator. It can be kept for a couple of days if the water is changed daily. It is known locally as Soya Paneer and is available at larger grocery stores or health food stores. One can safely use paneer (cottage cheese) as a substitute.

Vegetable Stock

Vegetable stock is an important flavouring agent for most Chinese soups and gravies. In the traditional Chinese kitchen pot of hot liquid with all vegetables scraps is always kept ready for use because the stock gives the body to the soups and gravies. However, if you do not have stock ready or feel lazy to make a stock, you can use seasoning cubes mixed in water instead.

Wonton Wrappers

These thin, soft squares of dough are made with flour and water. They are filled with vegetable mixtures and are then deep fried or steamed. You can make these at home as shown in recipe on page 141 or you can simply buy them. They are sold at leading provision stores either frozen or refrigerated. Samosa Pattis can be used as a substitute to wonton wrappers.

Soups

Starters

Vegetable Dishes 70

Simple Stir Fries 92

Noodles 100

Basic Recipes 137

Soups

Soups have a very important place in a Chinese meal. Soup is served along with the meal and serves as a beverage as the Chinese believe it is unhealthy to serve cold drinks with a meal.

Thin soups like Lemon Coriander Soup make aromatic appetizers and thick soups like Mein Chow Soup and Hot and Sour Soup make filling one-dish meals, particularly for lunch.

I am sure you will enjoy this selection of heart warming soups...

Spinach Soup

This light and healthy soup with mushrooms and spinach is just the right soup for spinach lovers. The sesame seeds add a nutty flavour to the soup.

PREP. TIME :
5 MINUTES.

COOKING TIME :
5 MINUTES.

SERVES 4.

2 cups spinach leaves, cut into big pieces
1 clove garlic, crushed
4½ cups clear vegetable stock, page 138
2 tablespoons dried black mushrooms (shitake), soaked
1 tablespoon soya sauce
½ tablespoon oil
salt and pepper to taste

For the topping
1 teaspoon sesame (til) seeds, toasted

1. Remove the stalks from the soaked mushrooms and discard.
2. Add the soaked mushrooms to the stock.
3. Heat the oil in another pan, add the garlic and sauté for 1 minute.
4. Add the spinach and sauté over a high flame for 1 more minute.
5. Add the stock, soya sauce, salt and pepper and bring to a boil. Simmer for 2 minutes.
6. Sprinkle the sesame seeds on top and serve hot.

You can use any other kind of mushrooms if you do not like dried black mushrooms. If you are using fresh button mushrooms, sauté them at step 4 along with the spinach and then proceed as per the recipe.

23

Cream Style Sweet Corn Soup

An easier way to make the ever popular Sweet Corn Soup and this recipe is completely fat-free. Even kids can rustle up this recipe with a little supervision….. of course.

PREP. TIME :
5 MINUTES.

COOKING TIME :
15 MINUTES.

SERVES 6.

1 can cream style corn (450 grams)
4 cups clear vegetable stock, page 138
2 tablespoons cornflour mixed with ¼ cup water
½ teaspoon Ajinomoto powder (optional)
½ teaspoon soya sauce
salt to taste

To serve
chillies in vinegar, page 134
chilli sauce
soya sauce

1. Boil the stock, add the cream style corn and mix well. Allow it to come to a boil.
2. Add the cornflour paste, Ajinomoto, soya sauce and salt and simmer for a few minutes.
   Serve hot with the chillies in vinegar, chilli sauce and soya sauce.

1) **Lemon Coriander Soup**, *page 32.*
2) **Steamed Chinese Bread**, *page 131.*

24

Chinese Vegetable Trio Soup

PREP. TIME :
5 MINUTES.

COOKING TIME :
5 MINUTES.

SERVES 4.

This clear soup has great eye appeal because of the different colours of vegetables used. The varied textures of the vegetables also add an interesting element to this soup. Feel free to choose any combination of your favourite 3 veggies.

4½ cups clear vegetable stock, page 138
¾ cup mushrooms, sliced
½ cup carrots, sliced
10 to 12 whole spinach leaves
½ teaspoon sesame (til) oil
salt to taste

To serve
chillies in vinegar, page 134

1. Put the stock to boil in a large pan.
2. Add the mushrooms and carrots and simmer till the vegetables are tender.
3. Add the spinach leaves and salt and boil for a few more seconds.
4. Trickle the oil on top.
   Serve hot with the chillies in vinegar.

1) **Chilli Coriander Fried Rice**, *page 121.*
2) **Kapi cho Potatoes**, *page 63.*
3) **Crackling Spinach**, *page 65.*

27

Mein Chow Soup

PREP. TIME :
15 MINUTES.

COOKING TIME :
10 MINUTES.

SERVES 4.

This is also known as Man Chow Soup at many popular eateries. An all time favourite, this soup is an ideal starter to any meal. The flavours of ginger and garlic merge beautifully with the fresh flavour of herbs like coriander and mint in this soya sauce based soup.

4½ cups clear vegetable stock , page 138
2 tablespoons tomatoes, finely chopped
2 tablespoons capsicum, finely chopped
2 tablespoons cauliflower, finely chopped
2 tablespoons carrots, finely chopped
2 tablespoons cabbage, finely chopped
a pinch Ajinomoto powder (optional)
2 teaspoons garlic, finely chopped
2 teaspoons ginger, chopped
1 tablespoon fresh mint leaves, finely chopped
1 tablespoon chopped coriander
3 teaspoons soya sauce
2 tablespoons cornflour mixed in ½ cup water
1 tablespoon oil
salt and pepper to taste

For the garnish
1 tablespoon chilli oil, page 144
1 tablespoon chopped coriander

1. Heat the oil in a wok over a high flame. Add the garlic, ginger, vegetables and Ajinomoto and stir fry for 2 to 3 minutes over a high flame.

2. Add the stock, mint, coriander, soya sauce and salt and pepper.
3. Add the cornflour paste to the soup and boil for 1 minute.
   Serve hot garnished with chilli oil and coriander.

Crispy Rice Soup

The crackle of the rice when added to this soup gives a sizzling start to your meal.

PREP. TIME :
10 MINUTES.

COOKING TIME :
10 MINUTES.

SERVES 4.

¾ cup cauliflower, finely chopped
¼ cup carrots, sliced
1 tablespoon celery, chopped
2 tablespoons spring onion whites, chopped
¼ teaspoon Ajinomoto powder (optional)
¼ cup tomatoes, cut into small pieces
2 tablespoons lettuce leaves, chopped
4 cups clear vegetable stock, page....
2 tablespoons oil
salt to taste

For the garnish
4 to 5 tablespoons crispy rice, page 143

To serve
chillies in vinegar, page 134
chilli sauce

1. Heat the oil in a wok over a high flame and add the cauliflower, carrots, celery, spring onion whites and Ajinomoto and sauté for 3 to 4 minutes.
2. Heat the stock, add the sautéed vegetables, tomato pieces, lettuce and salt and allow it to come to a boil.
3. Pour into a large serving bowl.
4. Just before serving, sprinkle the crispy rice on the soup and serve immediately with chillies in vinegar and chilli sauce.

Mushroom and Vermicelli Soup

An interesting combination of mushrooms and vermicelli. The dominant flavour of mushrooms is complemented with that of the bean curd while the rice vermicelli adds a contrast in texture to this simple but delicious soup.

PREP. TIME :
10 MINUTES.

COOKING TIME :
10 MINUTES.

SERVES 4.

For the soup
½ cup mushrooms, sliced
½ cup rice vermicelli
½ cup soya bean curd (tofu), shredded
2 tablespoons soya sauce
2 spring onions, finely chopped
1 teaspoon ginger, finely chopped
5 cups clear vegetable stock, page 138

For the garnish
2 teaspoons sesame (til) oil
1 tablespoon chopped coriander

1. Combine all the ingredients for the soup in a pot and bring to a boil.
2. Simmer for 5 minutes.
   Serve hot, garnished with the sesame oil and coriander.

If you cannot find soya bean curd, feel free to use paneer instead.

Wonton Soup

This soup is healthy without being heavy and is as enjoyable in summer as it is in winter.

The steamed wontons just melt in the mouth to release the crunchy vegetable filling. The spinach adds to the colour and the nutrient value of this soup.

PREP. TIME :
20 MINUTES.

COOKING TIME :
15 MINUTES.

SERVES 4.

8 steamed wontons, page 41
2 cups spinach, shredded
1 tablespoon celery, chopped
1 tablespoon garlic, chopped
1 tablespoon ginger, chopped
¼ cup spring onion whites, chopped
¼ cup spring onion greens, chopped
4 cups clear vegetable stock, page 138
1 tablespoon oil
salt to taste

1. Heat the oil and add the celery, garlic, ginger, spring onion whites and sauté for a few seconds.
2. Add the stock and allow it to boil for a few minutes.
3. Add the spinach, spring onion greens and salt and take off the flame.
4. Place 2 steamed wontons in each of the four soup bowls, pour the boiling hot soup over them and serve immediately.

You can use pakchoi or lettuce leaves instead of the spinach.

Lemon Coriander Soup

Picture on page 25

PREP. TIME :
10 MINUTES.

COOKING TIME :
15 MINUTES.

SERVES 4.

A fragrant and healthy soup. Fragrant lemon grass and piquant chillies make this clear soup very appetising. Coriander lends its own distinctive flavour and freshness to make this one of my favourite soups.

For the stock
2 to 3 whole lemon grass stalks, washed
1 to 2 chillies, slit

Other ingredients
¼ cup carrots, sliced
¼ cup mushrooms, sliced
¼ cup cabbage, diced
¼ cup red cabbage, diced

¼ cup spring onion whites, sliced
2 tablespoons spring onion greens, chopped
1 teaspoon oil
salt and pepper to taste

For the garnish
1 tablespoon chopped coriander
1 teaspoon lemon juice

For the stock
1. Combine the lemon grass and chillies in a pan with 6 cups of water and bring to a boil.
2. Simmer till the water reduces to approximately 4 cups. Strain and keep the stock aside, discarding the lemon grass and chillies.

How to proceed
1. Heat the oil in a pan and add the carrots, mushrooms, cabbage, red cabbage and spring onion whites and sauté for 1 to 2 minutes.
2. Add the stock, salt and pepper and bring to a boil
3. Simmer till the vegetables are tender.
4. Add the spring onion greens and serve hot garnished with the coriander and lemon juice.

Sweet Corn Soup

An all time favourite!
The delicate flavour of corn makes this soup a favourite of many people. The vegetable soup variation adds a lot more nutrients. Enjoy this soup plain or spiked with chillies in vinegar.

PREP. TIME :
10 MINUTES.

COOKING TIME :
20 MINUTES.

SERVES 4.

¾ cup whole sweet corn kernels
¾ cup sweet corn, grated
5 cups clear vegetable stock, page 138
3 tablespoons cornflour mixed with ¼ cup water
1 teaspoon sugar (optional)
salt to taste

To serve
chillies in vinegar, page 134
soya sauce
chilli sauce

1. Put the stock in a pan and add the sweet corn kernels.
2. Cover and cook over a medium flame for approximately 10 minutes or till the corn is tender.
3. Add the grated corn and simmer for another 5 minutes. Add the cornflour paste and simmer for some more time.
4. Add the sugar and salt and serve hot with chillies in vinegar, soya sauce and chilli sauce.

VARIATION : **Sweet Corn Vegetable Soup**
Add ¼ cup of chopped boiled vegetables of your choice at step 3.

Hot and Sour Soup

A wonderful blend of hot and sour flavours, this soup is just the thing for a relaxed, cold evening.

PREP. TIME :
20 MINUTES.

COOKING TIME :
5 MINUTES.

SERVES 4.

⅓ cup cabbage, shredded
⅓ cup carrots, grated
⅓ cup cauliflower, finely chopped
⅓ cup spring onions, chopped
2 pinches Ajinomoto powder (optional)
3½ cups clear vegetable stock, page 138
2 tablespoons brown vinegar
1 tablespoon soya sauce
1 teaspoon chilli sauce
1 tablespoon chopped, coriander
3 tablespoons cornflour mixed with ½ cup water
2 tablespoons oil
salt and pepper to taste

For the garnish
1 tablespoon chopped coriander

1. Heat the oil in a wok over a high flame. Add the cabbage, carrots, cauliflower, spring onions and Ajinomoto and stir fry over a high flame for 2 minutes.
2. Add the stock, vinegar, soya sauce, chilli sauce, coriander, salt and pepper and simmer for 2 minutes.
3. Add the cornflour paste and boil for 3 to 4 minutes while stirring continuously.
   Serve hot, garnished with the coriander.

Starters

This section is a delectable collection of starters, both traditional favourites and some that we are not so familiar with. All of these are delightfully easy to make but it will look like you have spent hours fussing over them.

Serve starters with a selection of dips that will complement them. I have made appropriate suggestions for dips with each starter.

Sesame Fingers

One of the most popular Chinese starters. It is made with vegetables layered on toast, topped with sesame seeds and then deep fried.

PREP. TIME :
20 MINUTES.

COOKING TIME :
30 MINUTES.

SERVES 6.

10 to 12 bread slices

For the topping
½ cup spring onion whites, chopped
¼ cup spring onion greens, chopped
½ cup carrots, finely chopped (parboiled)
½ cup French beans, finely chopped
½ cup capsicum, finely chopped
2 tablespoons celery, finely chopped
½ teaspoon Ajinomoto powder (optional)
1 cup potatoes, boiled and grated
2 teaspoons soya sauce
1 teaspoon chilli powder
1 tablespoon oil
salt to taste

Other ingredients
½ cup plain flour (maida)
1 tablespoon sesame (til) seeds
oil for deep frying

To serve
chilli sauce

1. Heat one tablespoon of oil in a wok or frying pan over a high flame. Add the spring onion whites, carrots, French beans, capsicum, celery and Ajinomoto and stir fry for 3 to 4 minutes.
2. Add the potatoes, spring onion greens, soya sauce, chilli powder and salt and cook for a few more minutes. Cool the mixture.
3. Spread a little mixture on each bread slice and press well by hand to make an even layer.

How to proceed
1. Make a paste of the flour with ½ cup of water. Apply this paste over the vegetables.
2. Sprinkle the sesame seeds over the vegetables and press them down gently.
3. Deep fry the bread slices in hot oil over a medium flame until they are golden brown. Drain on absorbent paper.
4. Cut each slice into 4 long strips and arrange on a serving plate. Serve hot, dotted with the chilli sauce.

Corn Rolls

An ideal cocktail snack! Creamed corn filled in flattened bread slices and deep fried to perfection. This starter is made using cream style corn which is otherwise used only for making soup.

PREP. TIME :
10 MINUTES.

COOKING TIME :
20 MINUTES.

10 bread slices

MAKES 10 ROLLS.

For the filling
¾ cup cream style sweet corn
⅓ cup onions, chopped
1 green chilli, finely chopped

1 teaspoon soya sauce
¼ teaspoon Ajinomoto powder (optional)
2 tablespoons oil
salt and pepper to taste

Other ingredients
3 tablespoons plain flour (maida) mixed with 2 tablespoons water
oil for deep frying

To serve
chilli sauce

For the filling
1. Heat the oil and sauté the onions and green chilli for a few seconds.
2. Add the cream style sweet corn, soya sauce, Ajinomoto, salt and pepper. Mix well and cook till the mixture becomes dry. Cool completely.

How to proceed
1. Steam the bread slices for 1 minute and roll out each one using a rolling pin so that it becomes thin.
2. On the corner of each slice, spread a little filling and roll into a cylindrical shape.
3. Seal the edges of the rolls from all sides with a little flour paste.
4. Heat the oil, deep fry until golden brown and drain on absorbent paper.
5. Cut each roll into two and serve with chilli sauce.

Cauliflower in Schezuan Sauce

PREP. TIME :
20 MINUTES.

COOKING TIME :
15 MINUTES.

SERVES 4.

A tasty way to serve cauliflower for a snack. Even those who do not like this vegetable are sure to enjoy this crunchy and spicy tit bit.

2½ cups cauliflower florets
oil for deep frying

To be mixed into a thick batter

4 tablespoons plain flour (maida)
2 tablespoons cornflour
½ tablespoon oil
a little water
salt to taste

Other ingredients

½ teaspoon garlic, chopped
½ teaspoon ginger, finely chopped
½ teaspoon green chillies, finely chopped
1 tablespoon spring onion whites, chopped
3 to 4 tablespoons Schezuan sauce, page 133
1 tablespoon oil
salt to taste

For the garnish

¼ cup spring onion greens, chopped

1. Dip the cauliflower florets in the batter and deep fry over a medium flame until crisp. Drain on absorbent paper and keep aside.
2. Heat the oil in a wok or frying pan over a high flame. Add the garlic, ginger and green chillies and stir fry over a high flame for a few seconds.
3. Add the spring onion whites and sauté for a few more seconds.
4. Add the Schezuan sauce, fried cauliflower florets and salt and mix well. Serve immediately, garnished with the spring onion greens.

Steamed Wontons

No Chinese meal is complete without wontons. Deep fried, steamed or in a soup! These dainty creations are enjoyed by one and all and are also very easy to make.

PREP. TIME :
20 MINUTES.

COOKING TIME :
25 MINUTES.

MAKES
25 WONTONS.

For the wontons
1 recipe wonton wrappers, page 141
3 tablespoons plain flour (maida), mixed with ¼ cup of water

For the wonton stuffing
1 cup cabbage, finely chopped
¼ cup spring onion whites, finely chopped
½ cup carrots, grated
¾ cup bean sprouts
¾ cup boiled noodles, page 140
½ teaspoon Ajinomoto powder (optional)
1 teaspoon soya sauce
1 tablespoon oil
salt to taste

For the tempering

2 teaspoons garlic, chopped
2 tablespoons spring onion greens, chopped
½ teaspoon green chillies, chopped
1 tablespoon oil
salt to taste

To serve

green garlic sauce, page 134
Schezuan sauce, page 133

For the wonton stuffing

1. Heat the oil in a wok or frying pan over a high flame. Add the cabbage, spring onion whites, carrots, bean sprouts and Ajinomoto and stir fry over a high flame for 3 minutes.
2. Add the noodles, soya sauce and salt. Mix well. Cool and keep aside.

For the wontons

1. Roll out the wrapper dough into thin circles of about 750 mm. (3″) diameter.
2. Put a little stuffing in the centre of each dough circle, apply the flour paste along the edges and fold over to make a semi-circle. Bring the ends together and press. *Refer to diagram on the next page.*
3. Repeat with the remaining dough and stuffing to make the remaining wontons.

How to proceed

1. Arrange the wontons in a greased steamer dish and steam for 10
2. Prepare the tempering by heating the oil in a wok or frying pan over a high flame and stir frying the garlic, spring onion greens and green chillies for a few seconds. Add the salt and mix well.
3. Spoon out the tempering over the steamed wontons and toss them gently.
   Serve hot with the green garlic sauce and schezuan sauce.

VARIATION : **FRIED WONTONS**

You can also deep fry the wontons till golden brown in colour, instead of steaming them. Serve them with Schezuan sauce, page....

 Ready-made wonton wrappers or samosa patti can be also used instead of making the wrappers at home. They are easily available at most leading provision stores in the frozen foods section. Cut them out to the right size using an inverted katori or a cookie cutter.

Making of a Wonton

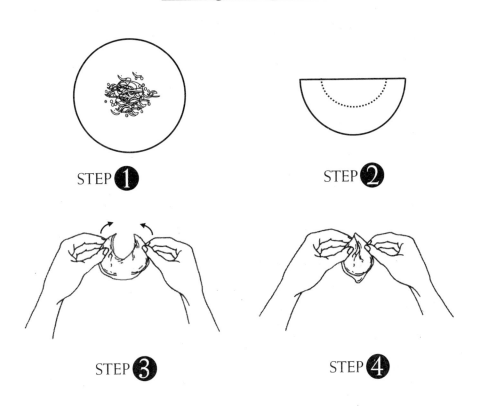

STEP ❶   STEP ❷

STEP ❸   STEP ❹

Crispy Fried Vegetables with Burnt Garlic

PREP. TIME :
15 MINUTES.

COOKING TIME :
15 MINUTES.

SERVES 4.

Golden fried crisp vegetables tossed with burnt garlic and spring onion is one of my favourite starters. These fried vegetables are best eaten immediately after they are cooked. Serve them with green onion and ginger dip, page 136, and Schezuan sauce, page 133.

For the crispy vegetables

3 cups vegetables (baby corn, capsicum, cabbage and cauliflower), cut into long strips
½ cup cornflour
½ cup plain flour (maida)
1 teaspoon ginger, grated
1 teaspoon garlic, grated
¼ teaspoon Ajinomoto powder (optional)
1 teaspoon lemon juice
salt and pepper to taste
oil for deep frying

Other ingredients

2 tablespoons garlic, finely chopped
½ cup spring onion whites, chopped
1 tablespoon oil
salt to taste

To serve

green onion and ginger dip, page 136
Schezuan sauce, page 133

For the crispy vegetables

1. In a bowl, combine all the ingredients except the vegetables and add enough water to make a thick batter.
2. Dip the vegetable strips in the batter and deep fry in hot oil till they are golden brown. Drain on absorbent paper and keep aside.

How to proceed

1. Heat the oil, add the garlic, sauté over a slow flame till the garlic turns golden brown in colour.
2. Add the spring onion whites and salt and stir fry for 1 minute.
3. Add the crispy fried vegetables and toss lightly. Serve immediately with the green onion and ginger dip or Schezuan sauce.

Onion Pancakes

**PREP. TIME :
10 MINUTES.**

**COOKING TIME :
20 MINUTES.**

**MAKES
6 PANCAKES.**

This is a real treat for vegetarians and non-vegetarians alike. Delight your guests with these delicate and fragrant green onion pancakes which are deceptively easy to make.

½ recipe wonton wrapper dough, page 141

For the filling

1 cup spring onion whites, chopped
1 cup spring onion greens, chopped
½ teaspoon Ajinomoto powder (optional)
a pinch sugar
1 tablespoon oil
salt to taste

Other ingredients
oil for deep frying
2 tablespoons cornflour mixed with ¼ cup water

To serve
green garlic sauce, page 134

For the filling
1. Heat the oil in a wok or frying pan over a high flame, add the spring onion whites and Ajinomoto and cook for 2 minutes.
2. Add the spring onion greens, sugar and salt and remove from the heat. Cool and keep aside.

How to proceed
1. Divide the dough in to 6 equal parts and roll out each portions into 125 mm. (5") diameter circles.
2. Place a spoonful of the onion mixture in the centre of each circle.
3. Fold the pancake as shown in the diagram on the facing page, sealing the edges with the cornflour paste.
4. Repeat with the remaining ingredients to make more pancakes.
5. Deep fry in hot oil till they are golden brown and drain on absorbent paper.
6. Cut each pancake into 2 and serve hot with the green garlic sauce.

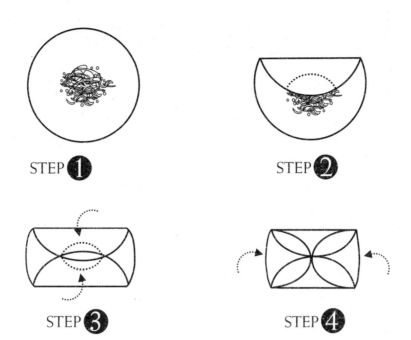

STEP ❶

STEP ❷

STEP ❸

STEP ❹

Spring Rolls

These tasty spring rolls are packed with lots of vegetables. They contain a lot of ingredients and are a little tedious to make but are worth the effort. Drain the filling thoroughly to ensure a dry, cohesive mixture and seal the rolls securely so they won't break open during frying.

PREP. TIME :
30 MINUTES.

COOKING TIME :
30 MINUTES.

MAKES 12 ROLLS.

For the stuffing
½ cup spring onion whites, chopped
1½ cups mixed vegetables (French beans, carrots, cabbage), cut into thin strips
¾ cup bean sprouts
¾ teaspoon Ajinomoto powder (optional)
½ cup boiled noodles, page 140
½ cup spring onion greens, chopped
2 teaspoons soya sauce
1 tablespoon oil
salt to taste

For the pancakes
½ cup plain flour (maida)
½ cup cornflour
¾ cup milk
2 teaspoons melted butter
a pinch salt

Other ingredients
3 tablespoons flour mixed with ¼ cup water
oil for deep frying

For the stuffing

1. Heat the oil in a wok or frying pan over a high flame. Add the spring onion whites, vegetables, bean sprouts and Ajinomoto and stir fry over a high flame for 3 to 4 minutes.
2. Add the noodles, spring onion greens, soya sauce and salt and cook for 2 more minutes. Cool and keep aside.

For the pancakes

1. Combine the plain flour, cornflour, milk, salt and ½ cup of water. Mix very well until no lumps remain.
2. Grease a 125 mm. (5 ") diameter non-stick pan with the butter.
3. Pour 2 tablespoons of the batter into the pan and tilt it around quickly so that the batter coats the pan evenly.
4. When the sides start to peel off, turn the pancake around and cook the other side for 30 seconds. Keep aside on a clean dry surface.
5. Repeat for the remaining batter to make 11 more pancakes, greasing the pan with butter when required.

How to proceed

1. Place one pancake on a dry surface and spoon a little of the stuffing mixture on the top end of the pancake.
2. Apply a little cornflour paste along the edges.
3. Fold the top and press firmly to seal, the mixture. Refer to Step 2 in the diagram on the following page.
4. Fold the left and the right sides of the pancake in order to get a rectangle. Refer to Step 3 in the diagram on the following page.
5. Roll the pancake tightly, sealing the ends securely with flour paste.
6. Repeat with the remaining ingredients to make the remaining spring rolls.
7. Deep fry in hot oil till they are golden brown. Drain on absorbent paper.
8. Cut each roll at an angle into two and serve hot.

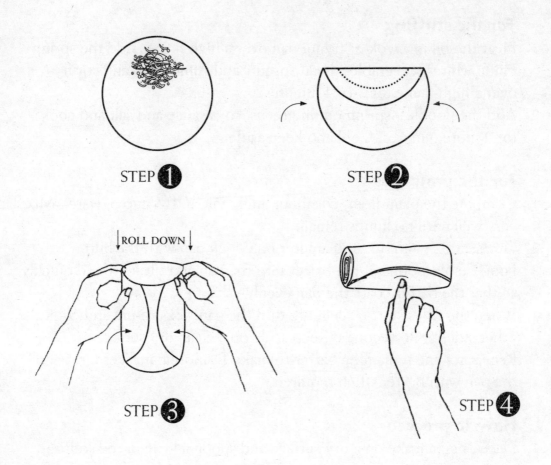

STEP **1**

STEP **2**

ROLL DOWN

STEP **3**

STEP **4**

1) **Singapore Rice Noodles,** *page 103.*

Dragon Rolls

Picture on facing page

These miniature little veggie filled wraps are a real hit. These small bite sized rolls make an ideal snack for cocktail parties. They are named dragon rolls because they are as spicy as a dragon's fiery breath.

½ recipe wonton wrappers, page 141

For the filling
¼ cup red cabbage, shredded
¼ cup cabbage, shredded
¼ cup red pepper, sliced
¼ cup bean sprouts
¼ cup carrots, cut into thin strips
2 teaspoons garlic, finely chopped
a pinch sugar
a pinch Ajinomoto powder (optional)
1 to 2 tablespoons Schezuan sauce, page 133
1 tablespoon oil
salt to taste

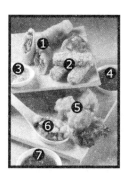

1) **Dragon Rolls**, *page 121.*
2) **Sesame Paneer**, *page 61.*
3) **Green Garlic Sauce**, *page 134.*
4) **Hot and Sweet Dip**, *page 61.*
5) **Lion's Head**, *page 55.*
6) **Pearly Corn**, *page 66.*
7) **Schezuan Sauce**, *page 133.*

Other ingredients

1 tablespoon plain flour (maida) mixed with
1 tablespoon water
oil for deep frying

To serve

green onion and ginger dip, page 136.

For the filling

1. Heat the oil, add the garlic and stir fry for a few seconds.
2. Add all the vegetables, sugar, Ajinomoto and salt and stir-fry over a high flame till the vegetables are tender.
3. Add the Schezuan sauce and mix well.
4. Remove from the fire and allow to cool completely.

How to proceed

1. Roll out the dough thinly into 100 mm (4") diameter circles.
2. Place a portion of the filling at one corner of rectangle. Roll up tightly starting from the end where the filling is placed to make a roll. Refer to the illustration on page 50.
3. Seal the edges using a little of the flour paste.
4. Repeat for the remaining rectangle pieces and filling to make more dragon rolls.
5. Deep fry in hot oil till golden brown and drain on absorbent paper. Serve hot with the green onion and ginger dip.

Lion's Head

Picture on page 52

These large potato and mushrooms balls coated with bread croutons are supposed to resemble the head of a lion. Traditionally, they are served on special occasions as they symbolize happiness.

PREP. TIME :
10 MINUTES.

COOKING TIME :
20 MINUTES.

MAKES 8 PIECES.

¾ cup potatoes, boiled and mashed
1 tablespoon onions, chopped
¼ cup mushrooms, finely chopped
1 teaspoon ginger, grated
1 small green chilli, finely chopped
2 tablespoons peanuts, crushed
¼ teaspoon soya sauce
¼ teaspoon Chinese 5 spice powder, page 146
1 teaspoon oil
salt to taste

To be mixed into a batter
4 tablespoons cornflour
4 tablespoons water
salt to taste

Other ingredients
3 bread slices
oil for deep frying

To serve
Schezuan sauce, page 133

1. Heat the oil in a wok or frying pan, add the onions, mushrooms and ginger and stir fry for 1 to 2 minutes.
2. Add the green chilli and peanuts and stir fry till the liquid from the mushrooms dries up.
3. Add the potatoes, soya sauce, Chinese 5 spice powder and salt and mix well.
4. Cool, divide into 8 equal rounds and keep aside.

How to proceed

1. Cut the bread slices into cubes of 12 mm. x 12 mm. (½" x ½").
2. Dip each potato round in the cornflour batter and then coat with the bread cubes. The bread cubes should cover the surface of the potato rounds.
3. Repeat with the remaining ingredients to make 7 more pieces.
4. Deep fry them in hot oil till they are golden brown and drain on absorbent paper.
   Serve hot with the Schezuan sauce.

PREP. TIME :
15 MINUTES.

COOKING TIME :
20 MINUTES.

SERVES 4.

Vegetable Balls in Hot Garlic Sauce

This starter is for those who like a little zing. The hot and sour garlic sauce which coats the deep fried vegetable balls makes a tantalizing starter or can even be served to make a snack.

For the vegetable balls
½ cup carrots, grated
½ cup cauliflower, grated
½ cup French beans, finely chopped
1 tablespoon cornflour
a pinch Ajinomoto powder (optional)
1 teaspoon oil
salt and pepper to taste

Other ingredients
oil for deep frying

To be mixed into a garlic sauce
1 teaspoon garlic, chopped
½ teaspoon ginger, finely chopped
½ teaspoon chilli, finely chopped
1 teaspoon white vinegar
1 teaspoon soya sauce
1 teaspoon vegetarian oyster sauce
¼ cup spring onion whites, finely chopped
1 teaspoon sesame (til) oil
¼ teaspoon pepper, crushed

¼ teaspoon cornflour

1½ tablespoons Schezuan sauce, page 133

1 teaspoon sugar

For the garnish
¾ cup spring onion greens, finely chopped

For the vegetable balls

1. Heat the oil in a pan. Add the carrots, cauliflower and French beans and cook till the vegetables are tender.
2. Add the Ajinomoto, salt and pepper. Sprinkle the cornflour and mix well.
3. Take off the flame and allow the mixture to cool.
4. Make 8 rounds from the mixture and keep aside.
5. Deep fry the rounds in hot oil till they are golden brown. Drain on absorbent paper.

How to proceed

1. Place the garlic sauce in a pan and allow it to come to a boil.
2. Just before serving, add the vegetable balls and bring to a boil. The sauce should be just enough to coat the vegetable balls. Add a little water, if required, to adjust the consistency.

Serve immediately, garnished with the spring onion greens.

Chilli Paneer

PREP. TIME :
10 MINUTES.

COOKING TIME :
30 MINUTES.

SERVES 4.

The traditionally non-vegetarian dish viz. chilli chicken is modified for vegetarians.
This melt in the mouth starter, made with paneer is flavoured with all the ethnic Chinese flavours is an all-time favourite that is really easy to prepare.
Serve it as a starter or even as accompaniment for your main meal.

¾ cup paneer (cottage cheese), cut into 12 mm. (½") thick strips
oil for deep frying

For the batter
¼ cup cornflour
¼ cup plain flour (maida)
1 teaspoon soya sauce
a pinch baking powder
salt to taste

Other ingredients
1 teaspoon ginger, grated
2 teaspoons garlic, chopped
2 teaspoons celery, chopped
¼ cup spring onion whites, chopped
2 to 3 green chillies, cut into 25 mm. (1") pieces
¼ cup capsicum, sliced
1 teaspoon soya sauce

1 teaspoon sugar
1 tablespoon cornflour mixed with 3 tablespoons water
1 teaspoon oil
salt to taste

For the garnish
½ cup spring onion greens, chopped

1. Combine all the ingredients for the batter in a bowl and make a smooth batter by adding approximately ¼ cup of water.
2. Coat the paneer pieces with the batter and deep fry in hot oil over a high flame till the paneer is golden brown.
3. Drain on absorbent paper and keep aside.

How to proceed
1. Heat the oil and add the ginger, garlic, celery, spring onion whites and green chillies and sauté over a high flame for 1 to 2 minutes.
2. Add the capsicum and sauté for a few more seconds.
3. Add the soya sauce, sugar, cornflour paste and salt and allow it to come to a boil.
4. Toss in the fried paneer and mix well.
   Serve immediately, garnished with the spring onion greens.

Sesame Paneer with Hot and Sweet Dip

Picture on page 52

PREP. TIME :
10 MINUTES.

COOKING TIME :
10 MINUTES.

SERVES 4.

Traditionally, this dish is made with tofu i.e. soya bean curd. This version uses paneer instead, coated with a sesame seed batter which imparts a nutty flavour and a very Chinese element to this crispy starter.

For the sesame paneer

200 gms. paneer (cottage cheese), cut into 75 mm. (3") x 12 mm (½ ") strips.
¼ cup cornflour
2 tablespoons plain flour (maida)
½ teaspoon soya sauce
½ cup sesame (til) seeds
salt to taste
oil for deep frying

For the hot and sweet dip

½ cup water
¼ cup sugar
½ teaspoon chilli powder
1 tablespoon lemon juice
1 teaspoon salt

For the sesame paneer

1. In a bowl, combine the cornflour, plain flour, soya sauce and salt with ¼ cup of water to make a smooth batter.
2. Dip the paneer pieces in the batter and coat the sesame seeds and deep fry in hot oil, till they are golden brown.

3. Drain on absorbent paper and serve hot.

For the hot and sweet dip
1. Place the sugar and water in a pan and bring to a boil.
2. Cook till the syrup is of a 2 string consistency.
3. Add the chilli powder, lemon juice and salt and mix well.
4. Cool completely and serve with the fried sesame paneer.

To get the authentic Chinese flavour, substitute paneer with soya bean curd (tofu).

Crispy Okra

PREP. TIME :
10 MINUTES.

COOKING TIME :
10 MINUTES.

SERVES 4.

Did you know that okra (bhindi) is one of the staple vegetables in Chinese cooking.
This recipe makes an interesting starter that's innovative and economical.
Deep fry the okra and store in an airtight container. Just before you wish to serve them, saute with the other ingredients.

3 cups okra (bhindi), cut into 12 mm. (½") pieces
1 tablespoon cornflour
oil for deep frying

Other ingredients
2 tablespoons garlic, finely chopped
¼ cup spring onion whites, finely chopped
1 to 2 green chillies, finely chopped

½ teaspoon soya sauce
1 teaspoon oil
salt to taste

For the garnish
¼ cup spring onion greens, finely chopped

1. Dust the okra with a little cornflour and deep fry in hot oil till crisp.
2. Drain on absorbent paper and keep aside.
3. In a pan, heat the oil and stir fry the garlic, spring onion whites and green chillies.
4. Add the fried okra, soya sauce and salt. Stir fry for about 2 minutes. Serve immediately, garnished with the spring onion greens.

You can also add a little Schezwan sauce to this recipe if you like to make a spicy variation.

Kapi Cho Potatoes

Picture on page 26

This sweet and sour potato preparation can be served as a main dish as well as a starter. The crinkle cut potatoes enhance the visual appeal of this delicious potato preparation. You can cut them like french fries, if you prefer or even cut them into cubes.

PREP. TIME :
10 MINUTES.

COOKING TIME :
10 MINUTES.

SERVES 4.

4 large potatoes, peeled
1 teaspoon garlic, chopped

½ teaspoon ginger, chopped
1 teaspoon green chillies, chopped
1 teaspoon tomato ketchup
2 tablespoons soya sauce
½ teaspoon chilli sauce
2 teaspoons cornflour mixed with ½ cup water
4 tablespoons oil
salt to taste

For the garnish
½ cup spring onion greens, chopped

1. Cut the potatoes into fingers using a serrated knife (scallop cutter) to get the crinkled shape.
2. Parboil the potatoes in salted water till they are almost done.
3. Heat the oil in a wok or frying pan on a high flame. Add the potato fingers and cook over a high flame for a few minutes till the potatoes are cooked. Remove and keep aside.
4. In the same oil, add the garlic, ginger and green chillies and stir fry for a few seconds. Add the potato fingers, tomato ketchup, soya sauce, chilli sauce and salt and mix well.
5. Add the cornflour paste to the mixture and cook for 1 to 2 minutes. Serve hot, garnished with the spring onion greens.

Crackling Spinach

Picture on page 26

As the name suggests this spinach crackles in your mouth.
Even those who do not care much for spinach are sure to like
this deep fried shredded spinach enlivened with sesame seeds.

PREP. TIME :
10 MINUTES.

COOKING TIME :
10 MINUTES.

SERVES 4.

4 cups spinach, finely shredded
4 teaspoons sesame (til) seeds
4 teaspoons garlic, chopped
2 teaspoons sugar
1 teaspoon oil
salt to taste
oil for deep frying

1. Place the shredded spinach in a metal strainer and dip it in hot oil till
   it is crisp. (This saves the hassle of gathering the shredded spinach
   from the hot oil.)
2. Drain the fried spinach on absorbent paper to soak all the excess oil.
3. Heat 1 teaspoon of oil in a pan. Add the garlic and sesame seeds and
   allow the sesame seeds to crackle.
4. Add the fried spinach, sugar and salt and mix very lightly.
   Serve immediately.

1. *To get crisp spinach, dry the spinach leaves individually*
   and then shred them finely using a very sharp knife.
2. *Do not heat the oil too much as the shredded spinach tends*
   to burn quickly.

Pearly Corn

Picture on page 52

Batter fried corn kernels, served sprinkled with spring onions and tomatoes.

These corn tit-bits look like small pearls when fried. This lovely preparation can be enjoyed even as an accompaniment to rice and noodles.

**PREP. TIME :
10 MINUTES.**

**COOKING TIME :
15 MINUTES.**

SERVES 4.

1 cup sweet corn kernels
½ cup plain flour (maida)
¼ cup cornflour
½ teaspoon readymade mustard paste
1 teaspoon chilli powder
½ cup water
salt and pepper to taste
oil for deep frying

For the garnish

2 tablespoons spring onion greens, chopped
1 teaspoon tomatoes, chopped (optional)

1. Mix together all the ingredients except the oil in a bowl and keep aside.
2. Heat the oil in a kadhai and scatter individual batter coated kernels in the oil. Deep fry until they are golden in colour and then drain on absorbent paper.

Serve immediately, garnished with the spring onion greens and tomatoes.

Creamed Corn Cakes

Delicious cutlets, crispy on the outside and smooth and creamy on the inside.

PREP. TIME :
5 MINUTES.

COOKING TIME :
30 MINUTES.

MAKES
25 CORN CAKES.

For the sweet corn cakes

1 can (400 grams) cream style sweet corn
4½ tablespoons cornflour
salt to taste

To be mixed into a batter

¼ cup plain flour (maida)
¾ cup cornflour
½ cup water
salt to taste

Other ingredients

oil for greasing and deep frying

To serve

green onion and ginger dip, page 136
Schezuan sauce, page 133

For the sweet corn cakes

1. Mix together the cream style sweet corn, cornflour and salt and blend in a liquidizer to make a smooth paste.
2. Pour into a greased 180 mm. (7″) diameter thali and steam for 10 minutes.
3. Remove from the steamer, cool and cut into 25 mm. x 25 mm. (1″ x 1″) square pieces. Keep aside.

How to proceed

1. Dip the sweet corn cakes in the batter and deep fry in hot oil till they are golden brown.
2. Drain on absorbent paper.
   Serve hot with the green onion and ginger dip and Schezuan sauce.

Vegetable Gold Coin

PREP. TIME :
20 MINUTES.

COOKING TIME :
30 MINUTES.

MAKES
20 GOLD COINS.

This snack looks like a small gold coin because of the appealing golden colour it gets from deep frying. It is an ideal snack for all occasions as the crisp fried bread topped with a mixture of potatoes and vegetable makes a mouth watering combination.

10 large bread slices

For the filling

½ cup spring onion whites, chopped

¾ cup carrots, chopped

¾ cup French beans, chopped

¼ cup capsicum, chopped

1 tablespoon celery, chopped

1 cup potatoes, boiled and mashed

½ teaspoon Ajinomoto powder (optional)

2 teaspoons soya sauce

1 teaspoon chilli powder

½ cup spring onion greens, chopped

2 teaspoons oil

salt to taste

Other ingredients

¾ cup plain flour (maida) mixed with ½ cup water
bread crumbs as required
oil for deep frying

To serve

chilli sauce

For the filling

1. Heat the oil thoroughly in a vessel and add the spring onion whites, carrots, French beans, capsicum, celery and Ajinomoto. Cook over a high flame for 3 to 4 minutes till all the liquid evaporates.
2. Add the potatoes, soya sauce, chilli powder, spring onion greens and salt and cook for 2 to 3 minutes. Cool the mixture.

How to proceed

1. Cut out 2 circles from each bread slices using a biscuit cutter.
2. Spread a little of the filling mixture on each circle, and press well By hand.
3. Apply the flour paste over the vegetables.
4. Sprinkle bread crumbs over the vegetables.
5. Deep fry the bread circles in hot oil till they are golden brown.
6. Drain on absorbent paper and serve hot with chilli sauce.

Vegetable Dishes

The Chinese believe that vegetables are foods that are used to heal many ailments. The cabbage, for example is being used for ages by the Chinese to cure ailments related to stomach. Like wise, the dried black mushrooms (Shitake), are known to have certain chemicals that are known to help cure hypertension.

In this section on vegetables I have included many recipes using different vegetables like cabbage, mushrooms, baby corn, ladies fingers, brinjal etc. which I am sure, even the ones who do not like vegetables, will thoroughly enjoy.

Creamy Vegetables

This dish is low in fat despite what the name "creamy" vegetables may suggest. Accompany these creamy vegetables with hot steamed rice to make a quick and wholesome meal.

PREP. TIME :
15 MINUTES.

COOKING TIME :
10 MINUTES.

SERVES 4.

1 cup cauliflower or broccoli florets (parboiled)
½ cup baby corn, sliced (parboiled)
¼ capsicum, sliced
¾ cup carrots, sliced (parboiled)
¼ cup spring onion whites, chopped
¼ cup cucumber, sliced diagonally
¼ teaspoon Ajinomoto powder (optional)
¼ cup milk
1 tablespoon cornflour mixed with ½ cup water
2 pinches sugar
1 tablespoon oil
salt to taste

For the garnish
¼ cup spring onion greens, chopped

1. Heat the oil in a wok or frying pan over a high flame. Add the cauliflower, baby corn, capsicum, carrots, spring onion whites, cucumber and Ajinomoto and stir fry over a high flame for 2 minutes.
2. Mix the milk and cornflour paste. Add to the vegetables and cook for 1 minute. If the mixture is too thick, add a little water.
3. Add the sugar and salt and simmer for a few minutes.
4. Garnish with the spring onion greens and serve hot with steamed rice.

Vegetable Hong Kong Style

This spicy vegetable preparation is a common favourite of many people. Accompany it with Celery and Black Pepper Rice, page 120 , for an excellent meal combination.

PREP. TIME :
10 MINUTES.

COOKING TIME :
5 MINUTES.

SERVES 4.

2 cups mixed vegetables (carrots, French beans, baby corn), diced (parboiled)
1 capsicum, cut into big pieces
2 teaspoons ginger, finely chopped
1 teaspoon garlic, finely chopped
3 to 4 dry red chillies, broken into pieces
2 pinches Ajinomoto powder (optional)
2 tablespoons soya sauce
2 teaspoons white vinegar
2 teaspoons chilli sauce
1½ cups clear vegetable stock, page 138, or water
2 tablespoons cornflour mixed with ¼ cup water
a pinch sugar
2 tablespoons oil
salt and pepper to taste

1. Heat the oil in a wok or frying pan on a high flame. Add the vegetables, capsicum, ginger, garlic, dry red chillies and Ajinomoto and stir fry over a high flame for 2 minutes.
2. Add the soya sauce, vinegar, chilli sauce, sugar, salt and pepper and mix well.
3. Add the cornflour paste and stock and simmer for some time, till the sauce thickens.
   Serve hot.

Vegetable Manchurian

This ever popular Chinese dish is really easy to make. When you eat these deep fried vegetable balls in a soya sauce based gravy, do not let mundane things like the weighing scale bother you! Just dig into these deep fried delights and enjoy !.

For the vegetable balls

3 cups cabbage, finely chopped
1¼ cups carrots, grated
⅓ cup onions, chopped
2 tablespoons cornflour
5 tablespoons plain flour (maida)
3 to 4 cloves garlic, finely chopped
1 green chilli, finely chopped
¼ teaspoon Ajinomoto powder (optional)
salt and pepper to taste
oil for deep frying

For the sauce

1 tablespoon garlic, finely chopped
2 teaspoons green chillies, finely chopped
2 teaspoons ginger, finely chopped
1 cup clear vegetable stock, page 138, or water
1 tablespoon soya sauce
1 tablespoon cornflour mixed with 1 cup water
2 pinches sugar
2 tablespoons oil
salt to taste

For the vegetable balls

1. Combine the cabbage, carrots, onions, cornflour, plain flour, garlic, green chilli, Ajinomoto, salt and pepper in a bowl. Mix well.
2. Shape spoonfuls of the mixture into small balls. If you find it difficult to form balls, sprinkle a little water to bind the mixture.
3. Deep fry in hot oil until golden brown. Drain on absorbent paper and keep aside.

For the sauce

1. Heat the oil in a wok or frying pan on a high flame. Add the garlic, green chillies and ginger and stir fry over a high flame for a few seconds.
2. Add the stock, soya sauce, cornflour paste, sugar and salt and simmer for a few minutes.

How to proceed

1. Just before serving, put the vegetable balls in the sauce and bring to a boil.
   Serve hot.

 Add some water or vegetable stock to thin down the sauce if it is too thick.

3 Treasure Vegetables

Colourful, simple and tasty. If you like, you can use your favourite combination of vegetables instead of the ones used in this recipe.

**PREP. TIME :
15 MINUTES.**

**COOKING TIME :
5 MINUTES.**

SERVES 4.

¾ cup asparagus, cut into 50 mm. (2") long pieces and blanched
¾ cup baby corn cut into wedges (parboiled)
¾ cup dried black mushrooms (shitake), soaked and sliced
¾ cup milk
1 tablespoon cornflour mixed with ½ cup water
2 pinches sugar
1 tablespoon oil
salt to taste

1. Heat the oil and stir fry the vegetables with salt. Keep aside.
2. Arrange the asparagus, baby corn and mushrooms on a serving dish.
3. Combine the milk, cornflour paste, sugar and salt in a pan and simmer for 1 minute till the sauce thickens.
4. Pour the sauce over the stir fried vegetables and serve immediately.

Vegetable Chow-Chow

PREP. TIME :
15 MINUTES.

COOKING TIME :
10 MINUTES.

SERVES 4.

This is a surprisingly quick and economical dish. It is sure to tickle your taste buds. Assemble all the ingredients before you start the actual cooking.

¼ cup spring onion whites, chopped
1 tablespoon garlic, chopped
1 tablespoon celery, chopped
¼ cup carrots, sliced (parboiled)
¼ cup capsicum, sliced
½ cup cauliflower florets (parboiled)
½ cup cabbage, shredded
¼ cup French beans, cut into 25 mm. (1″) pieces
¼ cup cucumber, sliced
½ teaspoon Ajinomoto powder (optional)
1 tablespoon cornflour mixed with 1 cup water
1 teaspoon sugar
½ teaspoon soya sauce
1 tablespoon oil
salt to taste

1. Heat the oil, add the spring onion whites, garlic and celery and sauté over a high flame for a few seconds.
2. Add the carrots, capsicum, cauliflower, cabbage, French beans, cucumber and Ajinomoto and stir fry over a high flame for 2 to 3 minutes.
3. Add the cornflour paste, sugar, soya sauce and salt and simmer for 2 minutes.
Serve hot with Schezuan fried rice, page 118

Vegetables in Spicy Garlic Sauce

Picture on cover

A simple yet satisfying dish of vegetables tossed in a spicy garlic flavoured tomato sauce. Feel free to use any combination of vegetables you like.

PREP. TIME : 10 MINUTES.

COOKING TIME : 10 MINUTES.

SERVES 4.

1 cup broccoli / cauliflower florets (parboiled)
½ cup capsicum, cut into traingles.
½ cup baby corn, sliced (parboiled)
¼ cup carrots, sliced (parboiled)
½ cup asparagus, cut into 50 mm (2") pieces (parboiled)
2 teaspoons ginger, finely chopped
1 tablespoon garlic, finely chopped
1 teaspoon green chillies, finely chopped
a pinch Ajinomoto powder (optional)
1 cup Schezuan sauce for cooking, page 147
2 tablespoons tomato ketchup
a pinch sugar (optional)
2 tablespoons oil
salt to taste

1. Heat the oil in a wok or frying pan on a high flame. Add the ginger, garlic and green chillies and stir fry over a high flame for a few seconds.
2. Add the vegetables and Ajinomoto and sauté for a few minutes.
3. Add the Schezuan sauce for cooking , tomato ketchup, ½ cup water, sugar and salt and bring the sauce to a boil.
   Serve hot.

8 Treasure Vegetables

The number 8 is a lucky one for the Chinese and this dish is one made on auspicious occasions using a combination of eight vegetables tossed in a delicately flavoured sauce.

PREP. TIME :
15 MINUTES.

COOKING TIME :
25 MINUTES.

SERVES 4.

½ cup snow peas, cut into 2 vertically
½ cup baby corn, cut into 2 vertically
¼ cup dried black mushrooms (shitake), soaked
¼ cup fresh mushrooms, quartered
½ cup carrots, cut into thin strips
½ cup broccoli florets
½ cup asparagus, cut into 50 mm. (2 ") pieces
½ cup bean sprouts
¼ cup onions, chopped
1½ teaspoons garlic, finely chopped
1½ teaspoons oil
salt to taste

To be mixed into a sauce

½ teaspoon soya sauce
½ teaspoon sesame (til) oil
¼ cup water
1½ teaspoons cornflour
1 teaspoon hoisin sauce

1. Parboil the snow peas, baby corn, fresh mushrooms, carrots, broccoli and asparagus till they are tender.
2. Drain and immerse them in cold water to refresh them. Drain again and keep aside.

3. Heat the oil in another pan add the onions and garlic and sauté for 1 to 2 minutes.
4. Add the soaked black mushrooms, bean sprouts and sauté for another minute.
5. Add the parboiled vegetables and salt and stir fry over a high flame for a few minutes.
6. Add the sauce mixture and bring to a boil, stirring continuously. Serve immediately.

 To use dried black mushrooms (shitake), you have to soak them in water for at least half an hour. When soaked well, the mushrooms become soft. Discard the stalks and use the mushrooms as required.

They are available at a few grocery stores and vegetables vendors.

Vegetables in Mustard Sauce

Picture on page 86

This healthy vegetable dish is made interesting by cooking it in a bright yellow coloured mustard sauce which has the sharpness of mustard and the subtle flavour of white wine. Surprise your guests by serving this unusual Chinese delicacy.

PREP. TIME :
20 MINUTES.

COOKING TIME :
10 MINUTES.

SERVES 4.

¼ cup leeks, thickly sliced
½ cup baby corn, cut into wedges (parboiled)
½ cup broccoli florets (parboiled)
¼ cup carrots, sliced (parboiled)
½ cup soya bean curd (tofu), cut into 25 mm.(1″)slices
2 cups Chinese white sauce, page 145

1 teaspoon readymade mustard paste
½ teaspoon sugar
2 tablespoons oil
salt to taste

1. Mix together the Chinese white sauce and mustard paste and keep aside.
2. Heat the oil in a pan and stir fry the leeks over a high flame.
3. Add the baby corn, broccoli and carrots and sauté for some more time.
4. Add the soya bean curd, sugar, the Chinese white sauce and mustard mixture and salt and allow it to come to a boil.
   Serve immediately.

 Do not cook the mustard sauce for a long time as mustard turns bitter when heated for long.

Okra and Baby Corn in Chilli-Hoisin Sauce

Crispy fried okra and baby corn tossed in a tempting hoisin sauce.

PREP. TIME :
10 MINUTES.

COOKING TIME :
10 MINUTES.

SERVES 4.

1½ cups okra (bhindi), cut into long strips
½ cup baby corn, cut into wedges (parboiled)
½ cup onions, cut into 12 mm. (1″) cubes
1 fresh red chilli, sliced (optional)
1 cup pakchoi, cut into wedges
1 tablespoon hoisin sauce
1 tablespoon soya sauce

2 teaspoons chilli sauce
1 teaspoon cornflour mixed with ¼ cup water
1 teaspoon oil
salt to taste

Other ingredients
oil for deep frying

1. Mix together the hoisin sauce, soya sauce, chilli sauce and keep aside.
2. Deep fry the okra in hot oil till golden brown. Drain and keep aside.
3. Heat 1 teaspoon of oil in a pan and stir fry the onions for a few minutes.
4. Add the chilli and pakchoi and stir fry for a few seconds.
5. Add the baby corn and okra and sauté for half a minute.
6. Add the sauce mixture and salt and mix well.
7. Add the cornflour paste, stir over a high flame till the sauce thickens and coats the vegetables uniformly.
   Serve immediately.

 Hoisin sauce is a proprietory sauce which is available at all leading provision stores.

Broccoli and Paneer in Lemon Coriander Sauce

PREP. TIME : 10 MINUTES.

COOKING TIME : 10 MINUTES.

SERVES 4.

A real hit at all occasions. The lemon and coriander sauce when combined with broccoli and paneer is an irresistible combination. The grated lemon rind adds bursts of lemon flavour as you dig into this sumptuous dish.

1½ cups broccoli florets (parboiled)
1 cup paneer (cottage cheese), cut into 25 mm. (1″) thick strips
2 tablespoons chopped coriander
1 teaspoon lemon rind, grated
1 cup Chinese white sauce, page 145
1 teaspoon oil
salt to taste

1. Heat the oil in a pan, add the broccoli florets and salt and sauté for a few seconds over a high flame.
2. Add the Chinese white sauce, paneer, coriander and salt and cook for some more time.
3. Add some water, if required, to adjust consistency.
4. Take the pan off the heat, add the lemon rind and serve immediately.

While grating the lemon rind, be careful not to grate the white pith, as it imparts a bitter flavour to the dish.

Brinjal and Pakchoi in Blackbean Sauce

Tease and appease your tastebuds with this Chinese blackbean sauce. Brinjal, pakchoi and blackbean together make this a very traditional Chinese combination.
Use your own combination of vegetables if you are not a brinjal lover.

PREP. TIME :
15 MINUTES.

COOKING TIME :
20 MINUTES.

SERVES 4.

2 cups brinjals, cut into long strips
1 teaspoon cornflour
1 cup onions, diced
1 teaspoon garlic, chopped
1 teaspoon celery, chopped
1½ cups pakchoi
1 teaspoon oil
salt to taste

To be mixed into a sauce

1½ tablespoons blackbean sauce
1 teaspoon sugar
1 teaspoon cornflour mixed into ¼ cup of water

Other ingredients

oil for deep frying

1. Dust the brinjal strips with a little salt and cornflour and deep fry them in hot oil till they crisp and golden brown. Drain on absorbent paper and keep aside.

2. Heat 1 teaspoon of oil in another pan and stir fry the onions, garlic and celery over a high flame for a few minutes.
3. Add the pakchoi and sauté for 2 to 3 minutes.
4. Add the fried brinjal and salt and mix well.
5. Add the sauce mixture, mix well and bring to a boil. Serve immediately.

Blackbean sauce is a proprietary sauce that is available at most leading provision stores.

Vegetables in Spicy Almond Sauce

**PREP. TIME :
15 MINUTES.**

**COOKING TIME :
8 MINUTES.**

SERVES 4.

Chinese cooking depends on a blend of various ingredients and condiments rather than the taste of individual ingredients. This recipe is a good example of harmonious and subtle flavours marrying together to create a simple but stunning dish.

2 cups vegetables (baby corn, broccoli, carrots etc.), cut into wedges (parboiled)

Contd...

1) **Ingredients for Chinese 5 Spice Powder,** *page 146.*
2) **5 Spice Mushroom Rice,** page *119.*
3) **Schezuan Style Stir Fried Vegetables,** *page 95.*

1 teaspoon fresh red chillies, sliced
½ cup almonds, blanched, peeled and sliced
¼ cup bean sprouts
2 cups Chinese white sauce, page 145
1 tablespoon oil
salt to taste

1. Heat the oil, add the red chillies, almonds, bean sprouts and
   vegetables and sauté for a few seconds.
2. Add the Chinese white sauce and salt and bring to a boil.
   Serve immediately.

To blanch the almonds, boil water and take off the flame. Add almonds to the hot water and keep aside for 10 to 15 minutes. The skin will loosen thus making it easy to peel the almonds.

1) **Vegetables in Mustard Sauce**, *page 79.*

Saiwoo Vegetables

PREP. TIME :
20 MINUTES.

COOKING TIME :
15 MINUTES.

SERVES 4.

An interesting combination of honey, 5 spice powder and dry red chillies creates this delectable dish. Strips of batter fried vegetables are coated in this unusual sauce.

For the crispy vegetables
2 cups vegetables, shredded (carrots, baby corn, capsicum)
5 tablespoons cornflour mixed with 2 tablespoons water
oil for deep frying

For the honey-5 spice sauce
2 tablespoons honey
2 teaspoons soya sauce
a pinch Ajinomoto powder (optional)
½ teaspoon Chinese 5 spice powder, page…
2 teaspoons sugar
salt to taste

Other ingredients
½ cup spring onion whites, chopped
2 teaspoons garlic, chopped
2 tablespoons ginger, chopped
4 dry red chillies, broken
2 green chillies, sliced
2 tablespoons Schezuan sauce, page 133
¼ cup spring onion greens, chopped
2 tablespoons oil
salt to taste

For the crispy vegetables

1. Make a paste with the cornflour and water and add to the vegetables.
2. Mix lightly so that the batter coats the vegetables.
3. Deep fry the vegetables in hot oil until crisp. Remove, drain on absorbent paper and keep aside.

For the honey-5 spice sauce

1. Heat the honey over a low flame in a small pan.
2. Add the soya sauce, Ajinomoto, Chinese 5 spice powder, sugar and salt, mix well and keep aside.

How to proceed

1. Heat 2 tablespoons of oil, add the spring onion whites, garlic, ginger, and sauté for a few seconds.
2. Add the dry red chillies and green chillies and sauté till the red chillies turn brown.
3. Add the Schezuan sauce, honey-5 spice sauce and salt and cook for a few seconds.
4. Toss in the crispy fried vegetables and spring onion greens, mix well and serve immediately.

 Do not cook for a long time after adding the vegetables as they will get soggy.

Kung Pao Vegetables

PREP. TIME :
15 MINUTES.

COOKING TIME :
10 MINUTES.

Kung Pao is one of the most popular dishes form the Schezuan region. The charred dry red chillies provide the fiery taste to these vegetables. Traditionally, the chillies are eaten with the vegetables, but unless you like hot food, you may prefer to set them aside.

SERVES 4.

2 cups vegetables (carrots, baby corn, broccoli, snow peas), cut into wedges (parboiled)
6 dry red chillies, broken into 25 mm. (1") pieces
2 tablespoons ginger, chopped
2 tablespoons garlic, chopped
a pinch Ajinomoto powder (optional)
2 teaspoons soya sauce
2 teaspoons sugar
2 teaspoons cornflour mixed with ¼ cup water
½ teaspoon white vinegar
½ cup cashewnuts, fried
1 tablespoon oil
salt to taste

1. Heat the oil, add the dry red chillies and sauté until they turn brown over a medium flame.
2. Add the ginger and garlic and sauté for a few more seconds.
3. Add the vegetables, Ajinomoto, 2 cups of water, soya sauce, sugar and salt and allow it to come to a boil.
4. Add the cornflour paste and bring to a boil.
5. Finally add the vinegar and fried cashewnuts and mix well. Serve immediately.

Do not allow the chillies to burn because, if they burn, they release potent volatile oils which can sting the nose and eyes.

Simple Stir Fries

Stir frying is a cooking technique designed for quick cooking while retaining all the nutrients present in the ingredients. It creates a colourful blend of interesting textures and flavours, thus elevating cooking from a menial task to an "art".

It is necessary that the food should be cut into units of roughly the same shape, same size and same thickness to ensure even cooking of all ingredients. It is important to prepare all the ingredients before you start to cook, so that the actual cooking is quick and flavourful and is over in a matter of minutes.

Stir fries are very easy and delicious and can be served either with rice or noodles. These stir fries are named for their most prominent flavours.

Stir Fried French Beans and Garlic

Crunchy French beans, tossed with garlic make this a very healthy dish. You can even enjoy this stir fry as a starter.

PREP. TIME :
10 MINUTES.

COOKING TIME :
10 MINUTES.

SERVES 4.

4 cups French beans, cut diagonally

2 teaspoons garlic, finely chopped

1 teaspoon sugar

3 teaspoons soya sauce

1 tablespoon oil

salt to taste

1. Blanch the French beans in boiling salted water for a few minutes.
2. Drain and immerse in cold water to refresh them. This will help to retain its bright green colour.
3. Heat the oil in a wok or frying pan. Add the garlic and stir fry till it is lightly browned. Add the French beans and stir fry for 1 minute.
4. Add the sugar, soya sauce and salt and stir fry over a high flame for another minute.
   Serve immediately.

Use tender French beans for best results.

Sesame Asparagus Stir Fry

PREP. TIME : 5 MINUTES.

COOKING TIME : 10 MINUTES.

SERVES 4.

There can be nothing more appeasing to the taste buds than the combination of asparagus and sesame seeds cooked to perfection. Quick to make and yummy to eat is what rightly describes this stir fry.

4 cups asparagus, cut 50 mm. (2") long (blanched)
3 teaspoons garlic, chopped
2 teaspoons ginger, chopped
3 teaspoons soya sauce
3 teaspoons sesame (til) seeds, toasted
1 teaspoon cornflour mixed with ½ cup water
a pinch sugar
salt to taste
2 tablespoons oil

1. Heat the oil in a wok or a frying pan, add the garlic and ginger and stir fry over a high flame for a few seconds.
2. Add the soya sauce and asparagus and toss well.
3. Add the cornflour paste, sugar, salt and sesame seeds and cook for 1 to 2 minutes till the cornflour coats the asparagus.
   Serve immediately.

Schezuan Style Stir Fried Vegetables

Picture on page 85

Sizzle up any of your favourite vegetables as I have done in this recipe with a spicy Schezuan sauce.
Garnish this dish with deep-fried rice noodles as I have done in the picture on page 85 if you like.

PREP. TIME :
20 MINUTES.

COOKING TIME :
15 MINUTES.

SERVES 4.

½ cup cabbage, cut into cubes
½ cup spring onion whites, quartered
2 cups pakchoi, cut into wedges
¾ cup baby corn, cut into wedges (parboiled)
¾ cup broccoli florets (parboiled)
½ cup snow peas, each cut into 2 (parboiled)
½ cup capsicum, cut into wedges
¼ cup zuccini, sliced
4 dry red chillies, broken into pieces
4 teaspoons Schezuan sauce, page 133
2 teaspoons cornflour mixed with ½ cup water
a pinch sugar
1 tablespoon oil
salt to taste

1. Heat the oil in a wok or a frying pan, add the dry red chillies, cabbage and ¼ cup water and allow it to cook till the water evaporates and the cabbage is tender.
2. Add the spring onions whites, pakchoi and stir fry for another minute.
3. Add all the other vegetables and the Schezuan sauce and cook for a minute.
4. Add the cornflour paste, sugar and salt. Mix well and allow it to come to a boil.
   Serve immediately.

Stir Fried Cabbage with Schezuan Peppers

PREP. TIME :
10 MINUTES.

COOKING TIME :
15 MINUTES.

SERVES 4.

Schezuan peppercorns are known as Tirphal in Marathi and can be found at local baniya shops. They are used extensively in Goan cooking and along the Southern coast.
They are also used in Chinese cooking and in this dish, they add flavour to cabbage which is otherwise a bland vegetable.

3 cups cabbage, cut into 12 mm. (½") cubes
2 teaspoons Schezuan peppercorns (tirphal)
2 teaspoons ginger, chopped
2 dry red chillies, broken into pieces
3 tablespoons Schezuan sauce for cooking, page 147
1 tablespoon white wine
¼ teaspoon sugar
2 teaspoons cornflour mixed with ½ cup water
1 tablespoon oil
salt to taste

1. Heat the oil in a wok or a frying pan, add the Schezuan peppercorns, ginger and dry red chillies and stir fry for a few seconds.
2. Add the cabbage and 1¾ cups of water and allow it to cook till the cabbage is tender and the water evaporates.
3. Add the wine and cook on a high flame for a few seconds.
4. Add the Schezuan sauce, sugar and salt and allow it to come to a boil.
5. Add the cornflour paste and cook till the sauce thickens.
   Serve immediately.

Stir Fried Chinese Greens

PREP. TIME :
10 MINUTES.

COOKING TIME :
10 MINUTES.

SERVES 4.

All the vegetables used in this delicious and tempting stir fry are healthy. You can enjoy as much as you like without worrying about the weighing scale.

2 cups spinach leaves, washed and drained
½ cup bean sprouts
2 cups pakchoi, cut into wedges
1 cup Chinese white sauce, page 145
1 tablespoon oil
salt to taste

1. Heat the oil, add the bean sprouts and stir fry for a few seconds.
2. Add the spinach and pakchoi and stir fry on a high flame till the greens soften and turn to a bright green colour.
3. Add the Chinese white sauce and salt and allow it to come to a boil. Serve immediately.

For the stir fried Chinese greens, the spinach and pakchoi have to be a little crisp. The cooking should be done on a high flame to avoid the spinach and pakchoi from turning black.

Broccoli and Baby Corn Stir Fry

Broccoli and baby corn together make an interesting combination because they complement each other in appearance as well as taste. The cashewnuts add an element of crunch to this exciting mixture of vegetables.

PREP. TIME :
10 MINUTES.

COOKING TIME :
5 MINUTES.

SERVES 4.

¼ cup onions, cut into wedges
¼ cup capsicum, cut into wedges
1 cup broccoli florets (parboiled)
¼ cup baby corn, sliced diagonally (parboiled)
¼ cup French beans, cut diagonally (parboiled)
a few pieces cucumber, diagonally sliced
1 teaspoon garlic, finely chopped
1 tablespoon cornflour mixed with ¾ cup water
a pinch sugar
7 to 8 cashewnuts, lightly fried
1 tablespoon oil
salt and pepper to taste

1. Heat the oil in a wok or frying pan, add the garlic and stir fry over a high flame for a few seconds.
2. Add the onions, capsicum, broccoli, baby corn, French beans and cucumber and stir fry for 2 minutes.
3. Add the cornflour paste, sugar, salt and pepper and simmer till the sauce thickens.
   Serve hot, topped with the fried cashewnuts.

Stir Fried Paneer, Mushrooms and Capsicum

PREP. TIME :
15 MINUTES.

COOKING TIME :
10 MINUTES.

SERVES 4.

Chinese cooking stresses the importance of colours and textures and for this reason the Chinese consider cooking, to be an "art". This dish fulfills all the criteria. It is colourful, has plenty of interesting textures and of course flavours that, I am sure you will enjoy.

½ cup capsicum, sliced
1 cup cauliflower florets (parboiled)
1 cup mushrooms, sliced
1 cup paneer (cottage cheese), cut into cubes
¼ cup spring onion whites, chopped
1½ teaspoons garlic, grated
1½ teaspoons soya sauce
salt and pepper to taste
2 teaspoons oil

For the garnish
½ cup spring onion greens, chopped

1. Heat the oil, add the spring onion whites and garlic and stir fry over a high flame for a few seconds.
2. Add the capsicum, cauliflower, mushrooms and salt and stir fry for 2 to 3 minutes.
3. Add the paneer, pepper and soya sauce and mix well.
   Serve immediately, garnished with the spring onion greens.

Noodles

Long noodles are a symbol of longevity in China. It is no surprise that noodles are eaten by the young and old in anticipation of a long and healthy life.

The Chinese believe that every meal should contain an equal proportion of starch and vegetables. A starch group they rely on to provide this harmonious dietary balance is noodles.

Noodles are extremely versatile and are not only used to make interesting main courses, as we have done in this section, but also in soups, for garnish and to make desserts.

In China, making 'hand-pulled' noodles is an art involving holding the stretched out paste (of flour and water) in both hands and whirling it around several times. Then the paste is laid out on a board and folded and refolded repeatedly. Eventually, the paste is transformed into long and thin noodles.

While in China, it is still possible to watch vendors make hand-pulled noodles, today most noodles are made by machine.

Hakka Noodles

An all time favourite! Noodles tossed with garlic and vegetables or any other ingredients of your choice like mushrooms etc.

This celebrated Chinese dish gets its name from the Chinese province of Hakka. Restaurants in India do not add as much chilli as mentioned in this recipe, but we have stayed with the traditional recipe. Feel free to make it your way, if you are not fond of spicy food.

PREP. TIME :
10 MINUTES.

COOKING TIME :
5 MINUTES.

SERVES 4.

2 cups boiled noodles, page 140
2 teaspoons garlic, chopped
2 dry red chillies, broken into pieces
¾ cup cabbage, shredded
½ cup capsicum, finely sliced
¼ cup spring onion whites, chopped
2 tablespoons oil
salt to taste

For the garnish
½ cup spring onion greens, chopped

1. Heat the oil in a wok or frying pan over a high flame. Add the garlic and dry red chillies and stir fry over a high flame for a few seconds.
2. Add the cabbage, capsicum and spring onion whites and stir fry over a high flame for 2 minutes.
3. Add the noodles and salt, mix well and stir fry for 1 minute.
   Serve hot garnished with the spring onion greens.

Pan Fried Noodles

PREP. TIME :
10 MINUTES.

COOKING TIME :
5 MINUTES.

SERVES 6.

A meal by itself.
The evergreen combination of mushrooms and green peas
prepared the Chinese way and served on a bed of crispy pan
fried noodles makes a perfect main course.

3 cups boiled noodles, page 140
2 tablespoons oil

For the vegetables

2 cups mushrooms, sliced
1 cup green peas (parboiled)
1 tablespoon garlic, finely chopped
1 to 2 green chillies, finely chopped
3 to 4 teaspoons soya sauce
1 tablespoon cornflour mixed with ½ cup water
a pinch Ajinomoto powder (optional)
2 tablespoons oil
salt to taste

For the noodles

1. Heat the oil in a wok or large frying pan.
2. Spread the noodles and cook over a slow flame until the noodles are lightly browned at the bottom. Turn them over gently and cook the other side until the noodles are lightly browned.

For the vegetables

1. Heat the oil in a wok or frying pan on a high flame, add the garlic and green chillies and fry for a few seconds.
2. Add the mushrooms and green peas and sauté them for a few minutes.
3. Add the soya sauce, cornflour paste, Ajinomoto and salt and cook till the sauce thickens. Keep aside.

How to proceed

Transfer the noodles onto a serving plate and top with the vegetables. Serve immediately.

Singapore Rice Noodles

Picture on page 51

PREP. TIME : 10 MINUTES.

COOKING TIME : 10 MINUTES.

SERVES 4.

This Chinese dish has subtle flavours that are not native to China but have influences of Singapore style cooking which is a melting pot of many cooking styles, cultures and flavours. These translucent, pretty looking rice noodles will just melt in your mouth. Flavoured with Asian flavourings like cumin and coriander, these noodles are sure to satisfy your taste buds.

To be mixed together

1½ cups cooked rice noodles
½ cup bean sprouts
1 cup spring onion greens, chopped
¼ teaspoon cumin (jeera) powder
¼ teaspoon coriander (dhania) powder
a pinch turmeric powder (haldi)
1 tablespoon sesame (til) oil

Other ingredients

½ cup spring onion whites, sliced
1 teaspoon garlic, chopped
¼ cup carrots, cut into thin strips
¼ cup French beans, cut into thin strips
¼ cup red cabbage, shredded (optional)
¼ cup red pepper, sliced
¼ cup capsicum, sliced
1 teaspoon oil
salt to taste

1. Heat the oil in a wok and sauté the spring onion whites and garlic for a few seconds.
2. Add the carrots, French beans, red cabbage, red pepper, capsicum and salt and sauté for some time till the vegetables soften. Sprinkle some water if required.
3. Add the rice noodles mixed with the other ingredients and toss well over a high flame.
   Spoon out into a serving plate and serve immediately.

 To cook rice noodles, soak them in boiling hot water for 10 to 15 minutes or as the instructions on the package specify. Drain the water and immerse in cold water in order to arrest any further cooking. Drain and use as required.

Chilli Garlic Noodles

PREP. TIME :
10 MINUTES.

COOKING TIME :
5 MINUTES.

SERVES 4.

For those who love their noodles spicy! This preparation is a must for the chilli and garlic lovers and the fact that it is really simple to make, makes it an all time favourite. Serve these with Stir Fried Chinese Greens, page 97, for a soothing and colourful accompaniment.

2 cups boiled noodles, page 140
¼ cup spring onion greens, chopped
¼ teaspoon Ajinomoto powder (optional)
¼ cup Schezuan Sauce, page 133
1 tablespoon chilli oil, page 144
1 tablespoon oil
salt to taste

1. Heat the oil thoroughly in a large wok or pan.
2. Add the spring onion greens, Ajinomoto, noodles, Schezuan sauce and salt and sauté over a high flame for a few seconds.
3. Pour the chilli oil on top and toss well.
   Serve hot.

Tangy Capsicum Noodles

PREP. TIME :
10 minutes.

COOKING TIME :
15 minutes.

SERVES 4.

This noodle preparation is sure to keep your taste buds guessing! Lemon, sesame oil, soya sauce and ginger combine their flavours to the fullest make this noodle preparation a real hit.

2½ cups boiled noodles, page 140
1 cup capsicum (red, yellow and green), sliced
1 teaspoon celery, chopped
1 teaspoon ginger, grated
1 teaspoon oil
salt to taste

To be mixed into a sauce

1 tablespoon soya sauce
1 tablespoon lemon juice
1½ teaspoons sesame (til) oil
2 teaspoons sugar (optional)
2 tablespoons chopped coriander

For the garnish

1 teaspoon sesame (til) seeds, toasted

1. Heat the oil in a wok or frying pan, add the celery, ginger, capsicum and salt and sauté over a high flame for a few seconds.
2. Add the noodles and sauté them for a few seconds.
3. Add the sauce, mix well and serve immediately, garnished with the sesame seeds.

American Chop Suey

A delightful preparation of crispy noodles served with vegetables and a tangy sauce.
This recipe is not an authentic Chinese one, but an invention of Chinese restaurateurs in Western countries. One of the literal translations of this recipe means 'savoury mess'.

PREP. TIME :
30 MINUTES.

COOKING TIME :
10 MINUTES.

SERVES 4.

¾ cup boiled noodles, page 140
1½ cups crispy fried noodles, page 142
2 cups cabbage, shredded
½ cup onions, sliced
½ cup bean sprouts
½ cup French beans, cut diagonally (parboiled)
½ cup carrots, sliced (parboiled)
½ teaspoon Ajinomoto powder (optional)
1 teaspoon chilli sauce
1 tablespoon oil
salt to taste

To be mixed into a sauce

¼ cup brown vinegar
¼ cup sugar
¾ cup water
2 tablespoons cornflour
1 tablespoon soya sauce
4 tablespoons tomato ketchup

1. Combine all the ingredients for the sauce in a pan, mix well and bring to a boil. Cook until the sauce is thick. Keep aside.

2. Heat the oil in another pan and add the vegetables and Ajinomoto. Stir fry over a high flame for 3 to 4 minutes.
3. Add the prepared sauce, noodles, chilli sauce and salt and cook for a few minutes.
4. Add half of the fried noodles and mix well.
   Serve hot, topped with the remaining fried noodles.

Vegetable Chow Mein

PREP. TIME :
15 MINUTES.

COOKING TIME :
20 MINUTES.

SERVES 4.

A complete meal ! A perfect combination of all nutrients contributed by the vegetables and starch from the noodles. Flavoured with hoisin sauce, this chow mein brings out all the authentic flavours of Chinese cooking.

Chow mein is a style of preparing noodles separately and then topping them with a choice of ingredients. Here we have used carrots, baby corn and mushrooms.

For the noodles
1½ cups boiled noodles, page 140
1 tablespoon hoisin sauce
1 teaspoon sesame (til) oil

For the vegetables
½ cup onions, sliced
1 teaspoon ginger, grated
1 teaspoon garlic, chopped
1 teaspoon celery, chopped
¼ cup carrots, cut into thin strips

¼ cup baby corn, cut into 4 lengthwise
1 cup mushrooms, sliced
½ cup bean sprouts
1 teaspoon oil
salt to taste

To be mixed together into a sauce
2 tablespoons hoisin sauce
½ cup water
1 tablespoon cornflour

For the noodles
Mix together the hoisin sauce and the noodles. Keep aside.

For the vegetables
1. Heat the oil over a high flame and sauté the onions, ginger, garlic for a few seconds.
2. Add the carrots, baby corn, mushrooms and salt and sauté for 2 to 3 minutes till the vegetables soften.
3. Add the bean sprouts and sauce and bring to a boil. Keep aside.

How to proceed
1. In a non-stick 150 mm. (6") diameter pan, heat the sesame oil and add the noodles. Arrange evenly on the surface of the pan to make a pancake. Cook till the noodles are golden brown in colour and lightly crisp.
2. Carefully turn the noodles around cook over a low flame for 3 to 4 minutes and then slide them on a serving plate.
Serve immediately topped with the vegetables.

Taro Nest with Warm Salad

Picture on facing page

PREP. TIME :
20 MINUTES.

COOKING TIME :
20 MINUTES.

MAKES 2 NESTS.

A pretty looking golden brown noodle basket which looks like a nest that's filled with a warm, crunchy asparagus salad. The vegetarian oyster sauce and honey make a wonderful dressing for this tongue tickling meal.

For the taro nest
2 cups noodles (parboiled)
2 teaspoons cornflour
salt to taste
oil for deep frying

For the warm salad
¼ cup spring onion whites, sliced
1 teaspoon garlic, finely chopped
1 green chilli, chopped
½ teaspoon ginger, grated
6 to 8 asparagus, cut into 25 mm. (1") pieces (parboiled)
½ cup baby corn, sliced diagonally (parboiled)
½ cup capsicum, diced
½ cup snow peas, cut lengthwise (parboiled)

1) **Green Onions & Ginger Dip**, *page 136.*
2) **Chillies in Vinegar**, *page 134.*
3) **Taro Nest with Warm Salad**, *recipe above.*

½ cup French beans, cut diagonally (parboiled)
½ cup bean sprouts
1 tablespoon oil
salt to taste

To be mixed into a dressing
1 teaspoon soya sauce
1 teaspoon vegetarian oyster sauce
1½ teaspoons honey

For the garnish
1½ teaspoons sesame (til) seeds, toasted

For the taro nest
1. Spread the noodles on a kitchen towel and dab lightly to absorb all the moisture.
2. Sprinkle the cornflour and salt on the noodles and mix lightly. Divide into 2 equal portions.
3. Place half the noodles in a strainer to make a basket, along the mesh of the strainer.
4. Heat the oil, hold the noodles in the strainer on top and pour the hot oil in the strainer, using a ladle, to fry the basket.
5. Keep pouring the oil on all sides until the noodles are golden brown.
6. Remove carefully from the strainer and place on absorbent kitchen paper.
7. Repeat with the remaining noodles to make another nest.

Honeyed Noodles with Vanilla Ice-Cream, *page 124.*

For the warm salad

1. Heat the oil in a pan, add the spring onion whites, garlic, green chilli and ginger and sauté for a few seconds over a high flame.
2. Add the asparagus, capsicum, snow peas and French beans and sauté for 1 to 2 minutes.
3. Add the bean sprouts and salt and mix well.
   Remove from the flame and keep aside.

How to proceed

Just before serving, toss the dressing into the salad and place half the salad in one basket. Repeat to fill the other basket.
Serve immediately, garnished with the toasted sesame seeds.

Vegetarian oyster sauce is a proprietory sauce and is available at all leading provision stores.

Noodle Rösti with Asparagus in Mint Sauce

A subtly seasoned noodle pancake served with garden fresh asparagus in a mildly flavoured mint sauce.

PREP. TIME :
20 MINUTES.

COOKING TIME :
15 MINUTES.

MAKES 2 RÖSTIS.

For the rösti

2 cups noodles (parboiled)
1 teaspoon garlic, chopped
1 teaspoon ginger, chopped
1 teaspoon celery, chopped

½ red chilli, sliced
2 teaspoons spring onion greens, chopped
1 tablespoon oil
salt to taste

For the asparagus in mint sauce
8 to 10 asparagus, (parboiled)
1 tablespoon mint, finely chopped
1 tablespoon chopped coriander
1 cup Chinese white sauce, page 145
1 teaspoon oil
salt to taste

For the rösti
1. Heat the oil in a wok or a frying pan, add the ginger, garlic, celery and red chilli and sauté for a few seconds.
2. Add the noodles, spring onion greens and salt and mix all the ingredients together lightly in the pan. Remove and keep aside.
3. With the help of 2 spoons, arrange half the noodles in a non-stick pan to form a 100 mm. (4") diameter circle.
4. Drizzle a little oil and cook over a medium flame till the noodles are crisp.
5. Turn the noodle rösti and cook on the other side as well till it is crisp.
6. Slide onto a serving plate and keep aside.
7. Repeat to make another rösti.

For the asparagus in mint sauce
1. Heat the oil in a pan, add the asparagus and salt and sauté for a few seconds.
2. Add the white sauce, mint and coriander and allow it to come to a boil.
3. Place the asparagus on one side of each rösti top with the sauce and serve immediately.

Rice Dishes

To the Chinese, rice is a symbol of life. When you are a dinner guest, it is considered bad manners not to consume every grain of rice in your bowl.

The Chinese generally use long grained rice for various rice preparations as I have done in this section. You have to be very careful with the way the rice is cooked because that is what determines the end product…
the perfect fried rice.

The Chinese also use another variety of rice called the sticky rice which has a very high starch content. This rice is not boiled in water, like the ordinary rice but has to be steamed to get the perfect texture. I have not included the sticky rice in this book.

Vegetable Fried Rice

No Chinese meal is complete without fried rice or steamed rice. To keep the rice grains separate, spread the cooked rice grains on a tray and allow it to cool. Rub a little oil on the cooked rice and keep aside till you require it.

PREP. TIME :
15 MINUTES.

COOKING TIME :
30 MINUTES.

SERVES 4.

2 cups Chinese rice, page 139
½ cup French beans, cut diagonally into thin strips
½ cup carrots, cut into long thin strips
½ cup capsicum, cut into long thin strips
1 tablespoon celery, chopped
1 cup spring onion whites, sliced
1 teaspoon soya sauce
1 cup spring onion greens, chopped
a pinch Ajinomoto powder (optional)
1 tablespoon oil
salt to taste

1. Heat the oil in a pan, add the vegetables, celery, spring onion whites and Ajinomoto and sauté over a high flame for 3 to 4 minutes till the vegetables soften.
2. Add the rice, soya sauce, spring onion greens and salt. Mix well and sauté for 2 minutes.
   serve hot.

Schezuan Fried Rice

PREP. TIME :
15 MINUTES.

COOKING TIME :
10 MINUTES.

SERVES 4.

"Schezuan" denotes spice ..... and this dish is a delectable blend of spicy flavours that are sure to tease your palate.

2 cups Chinese rice, page 139
1 teaspoon garlic, chopped
2 teaspoons celery, chopped
1 cup vegetables (carrots, capsicum, cabbage), finely sliced
2 tablespoons Schezuan sauce, page 133
½ cup bean sprouts
1 tablespoon oil
salt to taste

1. Heat the oil, add the garlic and sauté till it turns golden in colour.
2. Add the celery and vegetables and sauté for 2 to 3 minutes.
3. Add the Schezuan sauce and cook for another minute.
4. Add the rice, bean sprouts and salt and mix well.
5. Toss for a few seconds till all the ingredients are mixed.
   Serve hot.

5 Spice Mushroom Rice

Picture on page 85

PREP. TIME :
15 MINUTES.

COOKING TIME :
10 MINUTES.

SERVES 4.

Mushrooms and Chinese 5 spice powder together make this rice a very traditional fare.
This dish is a delicate blend of flavours and textures that may not appeal to all, but it's a "must" for those who like to experiment beyond the conventional Chinese fried rice.

2 cups Chinese rice, page 139
⅓ cup mushrooms, sliced
½ cup dried black mushrooms (shitake), soaked and sliced
1 teaspoon Chinese 5 spice powder, page 146
a pinch sugar
2 tablespoons oil
salt to taste

1. Heat the oil, add the mushrooms and sauté till they are tender.
2. Add the dried black mushrooms and sauté for 2 to 3 more minutes.
3. Add the Chinese 5 spice powder and sauté for ½ minute.
4. Add the rice, sugar and salt and mix well.
   Serve hot.

Soak the dried mushrooms in hot water for 15 minutes. Remove and discard the stalk.

Celery and Black Pepper Rice

PREP. TIME :
15 MINUTES.

Aromatic and subtly flavoured, this rice dish is the perfect accompaniment for spicy dishes.

COOKING TIME :
8 MINUTES.

2 cups Chinese rice, page 139
1 teaspoon garlic, finely chopped
1½ tablespoons celery, chopped

SERVES 4.

½ cup bean sprouts
½ teaspoon freshly crushed pepper
2 tablespoons oil
salt to taste

1. Heat the oil in a pan, add the garlic and sauté till it is golden brown.
2. Add the celery and bean sprouts and sauté for another minute.
3. Add the rice and salt and mix lightly.
4. Cook till the rice is hot, sprinkle the freshly crushed pepper and mix well. Serve hot.

Chilli Coriander Fried Rice

Picture on page 26

Picture on page 26

PREP. TIME :
10 MINUTES.

COOKING TIME :
10 MINUTES.

SERVES 4.

A fiery combination of red and green chillies with vibrant green coriander leaves not only makes this rice a treat for the eyes but also for the palate. Serve this with a simple stir fry to make a satisfying meal.

2 cups Chinese rice, page 139
1 teaspoon garlic, finely chopped
1 red chilli, sliced
1 green chilli, sliced
1 teaspoon soya sauce
2 tablespoons coriander, chopped
1 tablespoon oil
salt to taste

1. Heat the oil, add the garlic and sauté for a few seconds.
2. Add the chillies and sauté for a few more seconds.
3. Add the soya sauce, rice, coriander and salt and mix well. Serve hot.

Desserts

While westerners traditionally end their evening meal with a fancy dessert, the Chinese prefer to eat fruit (a much healthier custom) and desserts do not feature prominently in Chinese cooking. I have however, put together a few of the Chinese desserts that are popular.

Date and Sesame Wontons

PREP. TIME :
30 MINUTES.

COOKING TIME :
20 MINUTES.

MAKES
25 WONTONS.

A delightfully innovative dessert of wonton wrappers filled with a nutty date mixture. This is one of my favourite Chinese desserts and I will not skip that mandatory scoop of ice-cream.

For the wontons
1 recipe wonton wrappers, page 140
⅓ cup milk
oil for deep frying

For the stuffing
¼ cup sesame (til) seeds
⅓ cup brown sugar
⅓ cup dates (khajur), finely chopped
1 tablespoon butter, softened

To serve
vanilla ice-cream
2 tablespoons powdered sugar

For the stuffing
1. Toast the sesame seeds over a medium flame until they are lightly browned. Cool.
2. Grind them coarsely and mix with the brown sugar, dates and butter. Keep aside.

How to proceed

1. Place about 1 teaspoon of the stuffing in the centre of each wonton wrapper.
2. Apply the milk along the edges and fold over to make a semi-circle. Bring the ends together and press to make a wonton. Refer to diagram on page 43.
3. Repeat with the remaining dough and stuffing to make more wontons.
4. Deep fry in hot oil until they are golden brown. Drain on absorbent paper.
5. Sprinkle the powdered sugar on top.
   Serve hot with vanilla ice-cream.

Honeyed Noodles with Vanilla Ice-Cream

Picture on page 112

PREP. TIME :
15 MINUTES.

COOKING TIME :
15 MINUTES.

SERVES 4.

Round up your meal with this lip-smacking dessert. Crispy fried noodles drizzled with honey is a hot and cold combination when served with a nice dollop of vanilla ice-cream. Even your kids will love the noodles. Traditionally this dish is called "Darsaan".

1 recipe crispy fried noodles, page 142

For the honey sauce

1 tablespoon sugar
2 tablespoons honey
1 teaspoon sesame (til) seeds, toasted

To serve
vanilla ice-cream

For the honey sauce
1. In a small vessel, combine the sugar with 1 teaspoon of water and heat over a slow flame.
2. When the sugar melts, add the honey and sesame seeds and mix well. Keep warm.

How to proceed
1. Place the crispy noodles on a large serving plate.
2. Reheat the honey sauce and drizzle over the noodles. Serve immediately with vanilla ice-cream.

PREP. TIME :
10 MINUTES.

COOKING TIME :
20 MINUTES.

SERVES 4.

Toffee Apples

This typical Chinese sweet of batter fried apples coated in crunchy caramel make a perfect ending to any meal.

For the batterfried apples
3 firm apples
½ cup plain flour (maida)
2 tablespoons cornflour
¼ teaspoon baking powder

For the caramel syrup
1 cup sugar
2 tablespoons oil
3 teaspoons sesame (til) seeds, toasted

Other ingredients

oil for deep frying

For the batterfried apples

1. Mix the plain flour, cornflour and baking powder in a bowl. Add water and stir into a smooth, thick batter.
2. Peel, core and cut the apples into bite-size pieces.
3. Coat the apple pieces evenly with the batter and deep fry in hot oil until they are golden brown. Drain on absorbent paper.

For the caramel syrup

1. Put the sugar, oil and ½ cup of water in a pan and cook over a high flame.
2. When the mixture begins to bubble, reduce the flame and allow it to caramalize without stirring. If required, shake the pan gently to prevent the sugar from burning around the edges of the pan.
3. When the syrup is light brown in colour, remove from the flame, add the sesame seeds and mix well. Keep warm.

How to proceed

1. Fill a serving bowl with ice-cubes and chilled water. Keep aside.
2. Dip the fried apple pieces in the caramel syrup and coat evenly.
3. Remove and immerse them in the bowl of ice-cubes and water. Keep for a few seconds till the caramel coating hardens. Drain thoroughly and serve immediately.

Sugar caramelizes very quickly. Remove it from the flame as soon as it starts to change colour. It will continue to brown even after it is removed off the flame.

Fried Bananas

An exotic way to prepare bananas.
This is practically a national snack among the migrant populations in South East Asia and is traditionally served with scoops of coconut ice-cream.

PREP. TIME :
10 MINUTES.

COOKING TIME :
10 MINUTES.

SERVES 4.

4 bananas, peeled and cut into halves, lengthwise

To be mixed into a batter
4 tablespoons plain flour (maida)
4 tablespoons rice flour
1 tablespoon cornflour
a pinch baking powder
½ cup water
a pinch salt

Other ingredients
oil for deep frying

To serve
2 tablespoons brown sugar
vanilla or coconut ice-cream

1. Dip the banana halves in the batter and deep fry in oil until golden brown. Drain on absorbent paper.
2. Sprinkle with the brown sugar and serve immediately with vanilla or coconut ice-cream.

Coconut Pancakes

PREP. TIME :
5 MINUTES.

COOKING TIME :
10 MINUTES.

MAKES
12 PANCAKES.

This is one of the simplest desserts to prepare because the pancakes can be made well ahead of time and stored refrigerated in an air-tight container. When required, simply put together the coconut filling and pancakes, deep fry and serve immediately.

For the pancakes
½ cup cornflour
½ cup plain flour (maida)
¾ cup milk
2 tablespoons melted butter or oil
a pinch salt

To be mixed into a filling
¾ cup fresh coconut, grated
¼ cup sugar
1 drop rose or vanilla essence (optional)
1 tablespoon sesame (til) seeds, toasted

Other ingredients
oil for deep frying

To serve
vanilla ice-cream

For the pancakes
1. Mix the plain flour, cornflour, milk, salt and ½ cup of water. Mix well so that no lumps remain.

2. Grease a 125 mm. (5") diameter non-stick pan with the butter.
3. Pour 2 tablespoons of the batter, tilt the pan around quickly so that the batter coats the pan evenly.
4. When the sides start to peel off, turn the pancake around and cook the other side for 30 seconds.
5. Repeat for the remaining batter to make more pancakes, greasing the pan with butter when required.

How to proceed

1. Spoon 1 tablespoon of the filling on each pancake and fold. Seal the edges by applying a little of the pancake mixture. Refer to page 50 for or an illustration.
2. Deep fry in hot oil till the pancakes are golden brown. Drain on absorbent paper.
   Serve immediately with vanilla ice-cream.

Accompaniments and Dips

Most of us can cook some basic Chinese dishes and we often wonder how the smaller dishes or accompaniments are made. I often come back from restaurant thinking, "I wonder how they make that dish". Whether it's something as simple as chillies in vinegar or a more elaborate steamed bread recipe. This section unravels a few of those simple but mysterious recipes. Consisting of a mouthwatering array of dips and accompaniments that are sure to enliven your meal. Whether it's all time favourites like Khimchi, the fiery Schezuan sauce or the more unusual green onion and ginger dip, you will find easy recipes that will add more flavours to your cooking.

Steamed Chinese Bread

Picture on page 25

Picture on page 25

**PREP. TIME :
60 MINUTES.**

**COOKING TIME :
15 MINUTES.**

**MAKES
10 PIECES.**

A common Chinese lunch accompaniment or snack. This soft steamed bread is slightly sweet and complements the Chinese dishes which have mixed, sweet and sour flavours.
It is ideal to mop up your favourite Chinese sauces.

2½ cups (500 grams) plain flour (maida)
2 teaspoons (10 grams) fresh yeast
2½ teaspoons sugar
1 tablespoon butter
1 teaspoon salt
oil for greasing

1. Sieve the flour. Make a well in the centre.
2. Add the fresh yeast and sugar. Pour ½ cup of warm water over it and wait for 5 minutes until froth comes on top.
3. Add the salt and butter and make a soft dough by adding more warm water.
4. Knead the dough very well for 5 to 7 minutes.
5. Cover the dough and keep it for at least ½ hour or till it doubles in volume.
6. When double in size, knead the dough again for 1 minute.
7. Divide the dough into 10 equal parts, make small balls and place them on a greased steamer tray.
8. Leave them aside for 20 to 25 minutes or till they are double in size.
9. Steam them for at least 15 minutes.
   Serve hot.

A good indication that the bread is cooked is when a wooden skewer inserted into the bread comes out clean.

Khimchi

**PREP. TIME :
5 MINUTES.**

NO COOKING

MAKES 1 CUP.

This crunchy sweet and spicy preparation is the first dish that arrives when you are dining at a Chinese restaurant. Khimchi is a general term for any preserved vegetables (that are usually eaten in the winter when vegetables are scarce). You can also use cucumber and carrots strips along with the cabbage. Just remember to adjust the other ingredients proportionately.

1 cup cabbage, cut into 25 mm. (1") dices
1 teaspoon chilli powder
1 tablespoon powdered sugar
1 tablespoon white vinegar
1 teaspoon salt

1. Combine all the ingredients in a bowl and mix well.
2. Keep aside for at least an hour before serving.

You can refrigerate this for a few days, stored in an air-tight container.

Schezuan Sauce

Picture on page 52

Picture on page 52

PREP. TIME :
5 MINUTES.

COOKING TIME :
5 MINUTES.

MAKES ¾ CUP.

A treat for spice lovers! Use the variety of chillies like Kashmiri or Begdi which are rich in colour and not very spicy.

12 to 15 dry red chillies, soaked in warm water
2 tablespoons garlic, chopped
6 tablespoons white vinegar
2 teaspoons sugar
2 tablespoons sesame (til) oil
1 teaspoon salt

1. Drain out all the water from the chillies and discard it.
2. Grind all ingredients except the oil in a blender to a fine paste. Keep aside.
3. Heat the oil to smoking point and pour over the chilli-garlic paste. Mix well, allow it to cool and store refrigerated in an air-tight container. Use as a dipping sauce.

Select bright red chillies for a rich flovoured sauce.

Chillies in Vinegar

Picture on page 111

**PREP. TIME :
A FEW MINUTES.**

Chillies add extra punch to the vinegar that's often served with Chinese food. I often make some and store in a large bottle.

NO COOKING.

6 to 7 green or red chillies, chopped
1 cup white vinegar

MAKES 1 CUP.

Add the green chillies to the vinegar. Store in an air-tight container.
Use as required.

Green Garlic Sauce

This tongue tickling sauce is a refreshing combination of coriander, garlic, green chillies and vinegar.

**PREP. TIME :
5 MINUTES.**

1 tablespoon chopped coriander
1 teaspoon green chillies, finely chopped
2 tablespoons fresh green garlic, finely chopped
1 tablespoon lemon juice
1 tablespoon powdered sugar

NO COOKING.

MAKES ½ CUP.

2 teaspoons white vinegar
salt to taste

1. Mix all the ingredients together in a bowl.
2. Adjust the sweetness as required. Store refrigerated in an air-tight container.
   Use as required.

 If fresh green garlic is not available use 1 tablespoon of finely chopped garlic instead and add 1 more tablespoon of chopped coriander.

Honey Chilli Sauce

A simple but delicious dip that is sure to tickle your taste buds.

PREP. TIME :
5 MINUTES.

NO COOKING.

MAKES 1 CUP.

1 cup honey
1 tablespoon lemon juice
2 fresh red chillies, sliced
2 green chillies, sliced

Mix together all the ingredients together and serve.

Green Onion and Ginger Dip

Picture on page 111

Picture on page 111

PREP. TIME :
10 MINUTES.

COOKING TIME :
10 MINUTES.

MAKES 1 CUP.

This tempting dip made with spring onions spiked with ginger is one of my favourites.
Try it and I am sure you will enjoy it too.
This dip is served at room temperature but if you need to store it, then it needs to be refrigerated in an air-tight container.

1 cup spring onions, finely chopped
3 tablespoons ginger, finely grated
1 teaspoon sugar
a pinch Ajinomoto powder (optional)
2 tablespoons oil
1 teaspoon salt

1. Combine all the ingredients except the oil in a metal bowl and mix well.
2. Heat the oil to boiling point, pour over the spring onion mixture and mix well again.
3. Allow it to cool completely and serve.

 Chop the spring onion greens and whites separately and then mix them together.

Basic Recipes

Clear Vegetable Stock

PREP. TIME :
5 MINUTES.

COOKING TIME :
20 MINUTES.

MAKES 4½ CUPS.

Chinese stock differs from French stock in the lack of spices. While a recipe for French stock might call for a pinch of thyme or a few garlic cloves, the Chinese believe spicing masks the flavor of the stock. Seasonings are added later, depending on what the individual recipe calls for. This stock is used for soups and sauces to add more flavour to them.

½ cup cabbage, roughly chopped
½ cup carrots, roughly chopped
¼ cup celery, chopped
2 tablespoons spring onions, chopped
3 to 4 cauliflower florets

1. Boil all the vegetables in 6 cups of water and simmer over a medium flame for 15 to 20 minutes, till it reduces to about 4½ cups.
2. Allow the vegetables to settle at the bottom of the vessel and pour out the stock. Discard the vegetables.
   Use as required.

Chinese Rice

The Chinese have developed the simple technique of rice making into an art. Each grain of the cooked rice is separate and it is this method of cooking the rice that yields the perfect fried rice.

PREP. TIME :
5 MINUTES.

COOKING TIME :
15 MINUTES.

MAKES 4 CUPS.

1 cup long grained rice
2 tablespoons oil
1 teaspoon salt

1. Wash the rice thoroughly and soak in 3 cups of water for 30 minutes. Drain and keep aside.
2. Boil 6 to 8 cups of water, add salt and 1 tablespoon of oil.
3. Add the rice to the boiling water. Cook till the rice is 85% cooked.
4. Pour into a colander and let the water drain out. Pour some cold water on the rice to arrest further cooking.
5. Let all the water from the rice drain out ensuring that the rice does not contain any moisture.
6. Add the remaining 1 tablespoon of oil and toss the rice in it.
7. Spread the cooked rice on a flat surface till it is cool.
   Use as required.

Boiled Noodles

**PREP. TIME :
5 MINUTES.**

**COOKING TIME :
10 MINUTES.**

MAKES 2 CUPS.

*The Chinese believe that every meal should contain an equal proportion of starch and vegetables. One starch group they rely on to provide this harmonious dietary balance is noodles.
Here again it's a simple technique and one has to just cook the noodles correctly to make a great noodle dish.*

½ packet (100 grams) Chinese noodles
2 tablespoons oil
salt to taste

1. Boil water and add 1 tablespoon oil and salt.
2. Add the noodles, allow the water to come to a boil, and then simmer till the noodles are cooked.
3. Remove from the fire and drain out all the water.
4. Pour some cold water on the noodles to arrest further cooking.
5. Let all the water drain out and ensure that the noodles do not contain any moisture.
6. Add the remaining 1 tablespoon of oil and mix lightly. This will prevent the noodles from sticking together. Use as required.

When the noodles are cooked they will rise to the top.

Wonton Wrappers and Crispy Noodles

This basic recipe unravels the mystery behind the ever so popular wontons and crispy noodles. The same dough can be used to make wontons as well as the crispy noodles.

PREP. TIME :
15 MINUTES.

COOKING TIME :
10 MINUTES.

MAKES
25 WONTONS.

1 cup plain flour (maida)
½ cup warm water
2 teaspoons oil
½ teaspoon salt

For the dough

1. Sieve the flour and salt together.
2. Add the water gradually and make a soft dough.
3. Add the oil and knead for a while. Keep aside for 30 minutes, covered with a damp muslin cloth.
4. Apply a few drops of oil on your palm and knead the dough until it becomes smooth and elastic.

For the wontons

1. Divide the dough into 25 equal portions.
2. Roll out each portion into a 75 mm. (3") in diameter circle. Use as required.

For the crispy noodles

1. Divide the dough into 6 equal portions.
2. Roll out each portion into a 150 mm. (6") diameter circle. Cut into strips 6 mm. (¼") thick and deep fry in hot oil until they are golden brown.
3. Drain on absorbent paper and use as required.

Wonton wrappers are also available at many leading provision stores in the frozen food section.

Crispy Fried Noodles

**PREP. TIME :
5 MINUTES.**

**COOKING TIME :
20 MINUTES.**

SERVES 4.

*Regular noodles that are parboiled and deep fried to be served as a topping on soups or as a principal ingredient in Chop Suey.
I enjoy these at the beginning of my Chinese meal, drizzled with Schezuan sauce, page 133.*

1 packet (200 grams) Chinese noodles
2 tablespoons oil
salt to taste
oil for deep frying

1. Boil 4 cups of water and add 2 tablespoons of oil. Add the noodles while stirring occasionally and cook until they are parboiled. Drain well.
2. Spread the noodles on a clean piece of cloth and allow to dry for at least 2 to 3 hours.
3. Heat plenty of oil in a wok or frying pan over a medium heat. Fry small quantities of noodles at a time in the hot oil until golden brown.
4. Remove the noodles from the oil and drain on absorbent paper.
5. Repeat with the remaining noodles. Use as required.

If the noodles still look a bit soft after drying, sprinkle a little cornflour over them and then deep fry.

Crispy Rice

PREP. TIME :
5 MINUTES.

COOKING TIME :
20 MINUTES.

MAKES 1½ CUPS.

This is partially cooked rice that is sun dried and stored. It is then deep fried just before serving. We have used these in the recipe of Crispy Rice Soup, page 29.

¾ cup long grained rice

1. Boil plenty of water in a pan. Add the rice and cook.
2. When the rice is 90% cooked, drain out all the water.
3. Spread the rice on a large tray, cover with a piece of cloth and sun dry until crisp.
4. Store in an air-tight container.
5. When required, place the dried rice in a strainer and deep fry for a few seconds till the rice puffs up. Drain on absorbent paper. Use immediately.

The dried rice lasts for 3 to 4 months, if stored in an airtight container.

Chilli Oil

A simple way of flavouring oil to add more flavours to our cooking. Chillies add a warm, pungent aroma to the oil.

PREP. TIME :
5 MINUTES.

COOKING TIME :
5 MINUTES.

15 to 20 dry red chillies
1 cup oil

MAKES 1 CUP.

1. Break the red chillies into big pieces.
2. Heat the oil to smoking point, add the chillies and switch off the gas.
3. Cover and keep aside for 2 hours. Strain and store the oil in a bottle, discarding the chillies. Use as required.

Chinese White Sauce

This simple sauce is one of the main sauces used in Chinese cuisine and forms the base for many authentic Chinese preparations. The white wine in the sauce lends the authentic Chinese flavour to this sauce. You may however exclude it from the recipe if you prefer.

**PREP. TIME :
10 MINUTES.**

**COOKING TIME :
10 MINUTES.**

MAKES 2 CUPS.

½ cup onions, finely chopped
2 teaspoons ginger, chopped
2 teaspoons garlic, chopped
½ cup white wine
2 tablespoons cornflour mixed with 3 cups clear vegetable stock, page 138, or water
a pinch sugar
1 tablespoon oil
salt to taste

1. Heat the oil in a pan, add the onions, ginger and garlic and sauté till the onions are translucent.
2. Add the wine and cook on a high flame for a few seconds.
3. Add the cornflour paste and simmer till the sauce thickens.
4. Add sugar and salt, mix well and use as required.
   Mix well and use as required.

Chinese 5 Spice Powder

PREP. TIME :
10 MINUTES.

COOKING TIME :
15 MINUTES.

MAKES ¼ CUP.

An authentic home-made version of the original blend of spices. Just like our very own garam masala, every Chinese household has it's own delicate balance of ingredients to make this fragrant powder. This is the one I learnt from a dear Chinese friend of mine.

4 teaspoons Schezuan peppercorns (tirphal)
16 whole star anise (chakri phool)
12 cloves (laung)
10 sticks cinnamon (dalchini)
2 tablespoons fennel seeds (saunf)

1. In a dry pan, roast the Schezuan peppercorns over low heat until the aroma is released. Keep aside.
2. Roast together the other ingredients for about 3 minutes on low heat till the aroma is released.
3. Grind together all the ingredients in a blender. Sieve the mixture.
4. A coarse powder of the spices will be left behind. Grind it again to make a fine powder and sieve again. Discard the coarse powder left behind or grind it again.
5. Store the sieved powder in an air-tight jar and use as required.

Schezuan Sauce for Cooking

PREP. TIME :
10 MINUTES.

COOKING TIME :
5 MINUTES.

MAKES 1 CUP.

This fiery sauce is one of my favourites. It is a delicate blend of fiery spices and condiments without which I am sure your Chinese cooking will be incomplete.

For the paste
20 dry red chillies
¼ cup garlic, chopped

Other ingredients
1 tablespoon garlic, finely chopped
1 teaspoon green chillies, finely chopped
½ tablespoon ginger, grated
2 tablespoons onions, finely chopped
1 teaspoon celery, finely chopped
1 cup clear vegetable stock, page…
1 tablespoon cornflour mixed with 2 tablespoons water
1 tablespoon white vinegar
2 teaspoons sugar
a pinch Ajinomoto powder (optional)
3 tablespoons oil
salt to taste

For the paste
1. Boil 1 cup of water.
2. Add the dry red chillies and garlic and simmer for 8 to 10 minutes. Cool.

3. Drain out the water. Grind into a smooth paste in a liquidiser using a little water.

How to proceed

1. Heat the oil in a wok or frying pan and sauté the garlic, green chillies, ginger, onions and celery for 1 minute.
2. Add the paste and sauté again for 1 minute.
3. Add the stock and mix well. Add the cornflour mixture, vinegar, sugar, Ajinomoto and salt. Bring to a boil and keep aside.
   Use as required.